Reflections

Shaykh Yasir Qadhi

Al Buruj Press
2023

Distributed and Published by Al Buruj Press.

Author: Yasir Qadhi

Distributed in the UK by Al Buruj Press.

Al Buruj Press
Masjid Ramadan
9 Shacklewell Lane
London
E8 2DA

Tel: +447947363946
Website:www.alburujpress.com
Email: info@alburujpress.com

Second Edition 2023

ISBN no: 978-1-915851-03-1

Publishers Comments

When the opportunity arose of potentially publishing this work, I immediately committed to it due to the value which I saw within it. As I read the work myself, it became clear to me that I needed to bring this work to life, as it has the potential to benefit thousands around the world.

Shaykh Yasir Qadhi needs no introduction. In my humble opinion, he is one of the most important western Muslim scholars of our time whom Allah has blessed with the quality of approaching the texts with an open and sincere mind. This book I believe provides a glimpse of the thoughts of the Shaykh as collected from several years of his public speaking. Indeed Allah blesses those who make a constant effort to unite the people of this ummah and bring them to eeman, especially during the present times where it is greatly needed.

I'd like to thank Sister Shaakirah whose initial collection of the speeches of the Shaykh helped us to start this work. Importantly, I ask Allah to bless my good friend, Dr Forid, who worked closely with me to analyse, extensively edit and present the book in the final version you find it now. May Allah reward him greatly for his noble efforts. We have tried to keep the book such that it is relevant to believers at any stage and age of their life, and simple to understand with the hope that the message resonates with all types of audience.

Finally, we ask Allah to bless our endeavours, forgive our parents and those beloved to us.

This day, I have completed your religion for you, perfected My blessings upon you, and am pleased with Islaam as your Religion. (Quran, 5:3)

In Allah's Trust,
Zayd ul Islam
Al Buruj Press Founder
Friday 13th November 2020 (27th Rabī' al-Awwal 1442)

Introduction

All praise be to the One whom, were He to be praised by all of the creation for all of eternity, would still be worthy of infinitely more praise! And may peace and salutations be on the one who was sent as a Mercy to the entire creation.

Life is a journey. Every one of us is gifted a set amount of time on this earth, and we all must make the best of it before that time is up. While none of us knows exactly how long we have, what is amazing is that per unit time, we all get the exact same amount every unit. We may get different total amounts, but no one's hour is discernably different from another person's hour. Yet, that is the only real similarity. Some people simply waste entire decades away, while others perform deeds in a few hours or even minutes that last for all of eternity! Some people live life so unremarkably that their existence and non-existence is almost the same to others; while some literally change the course of history.

This book is meant to inspire us all on this journey of life so that we make the best use of our time. Each topic is chosen to be a quick, easy read with a message that is useful to people at any stage of this journey. These topics were all chosen and selected from khuṭbahs and talks that I have given over the last almost three decades of public speaking, with extensive editing for content, along with the necessary stylistic editing and footnotes that a written work deserves.

I would like to thank Sr. Shaakirah Edwards for her help in collating and typing the first draft of the work, along with a special thanks to the editors and publishing team of Al Buruj Press, who worked tirelessly to present this work in the elegant manner that you now find it.

Of course, special mention must be made of my family. My three teenagers and one tween are now accustomed to leaving their father in his study for many, many hours; I hope that when they are adults, they can forgive the long absences their father had during their growing years. I hope they realize that while my time with them might not have been as much as other fathers, the love that I had for them was a constant motivation for me in my work. My wife of a quarter of a century has been my main support and pillar, and I thank Allah for such a wonderful 'Khadījah' figure in my life. I shall always be grateful to my parents for raising me upon the foundations of this faith and instilling in me the love of the Qur'ān, and for encouraging me to memorize the Book of Allah, and then to study Islam in the city of the Prophet (ﷺ). I am fortunate that they are now living with me, and that our proximity is a source of comfort to them: *"O Allah! Have mercy on them even as they reared me as a child" [Isrā: 24].*

I pray that this work will be a source of inspiration for all who read it, and a source of blessings for me on Judgment Day.

Dr. Yasir Qadhi
Plano, TX
29th October, 2020 CE (12th Rabī' al-Awwal, 1442 AH)

Contents

Publishers Comments 3

Introduction 5

1) Tree of Faith 8

2) Journey of Worship 16

3) Prayer 24

4) Quran 29

5) Love of the Prophet 37

6) Born Muslim 44

7) Hard Hearts 51

8) Crisis of Knowledge 60

9) The State We're In 68

10) Our Times, Our Challenges 74

11) Lost Faith 82

12) Fear of Others 89

13) The Wisdom of Pandemics 97

14) Patience 104

15) Arrogance and Humility 111

16) Forgiveness 119

17) Scholarship 126

18) Unity 135

19) Spouses 143

20) Next Generation 151

21) Legacy 159

Tree of Faith

1

Tree of Faith

أَلَمْ تَرَ كَيْفَ ضَرَبَ اللَّهُ مَثَلًا كَلِمَةً طَيِّبَةً كَشَجَرَةٍ طَيِّبَةٍ
أَصْلُهَا ثَابِتٌ وَفَرْعُهَا فِي السَّمَاءِ
تُؤْتِي أُكُلَهَا كُلَّ حِينٍ بِإِذْنِ رَبِّهَا ۗ وَيَضْرِبُ اللَّهُ الْأَمْثَالَ
لِلنَّاسِ لَعَلَّهُمْ يَتَذَكَّرُونَ

"Have you not considered how Allah sets forth a parable?
Making a good word like a good tree,
whose root is firmly fixed and its branches high in the sky?
It produces fruits all the time, by the permission of its Lord.
And Allah presents examples for mankind,
that perhaps they may be reminded."

(*Ibrāhīm* 14: 24-25)

Allah presents for us this eloquent parable of a good word being comparable to that of a good tree. The 'good word' being referred to here is the *kalimah ṭayyibah*: our testimony of faith. Allah compares our faith to a beautiful tree. The roots of this tree are deep, making its foundations firm, and its branches are towering high in the sky. He tells us that this tree gives us fruits at every time of the year; it is evergreen and ever fruitful, by the permission of its Lord. Allah commands us to think about this example that He has given, so what benefits can we derive?

The symbolism Allah uses for our faith is extremely profound. In every culture around the world, the tree symbolises life. It provides humans with all the necessary elements to live: wood for shelter and fuel, shade for protection and fruits to eat. Furthermore, its leaves take in carbon dioxide and convert it into oxygen which we are then able to breathe to sustain our existence. This process of photosynthesis is where the cycle of life begins. Without it, our entire ecosystem would collapse. Similarly, our testimony of faith is the spiritual building block that gives life to everything else.

As well as this, the tree also symbolises strength. Allah tells us that this tree is firm; its roots go deep into the ground. Whenever there are hurricanes or tornados, houses collapse and cars turn over, but we will rarely find a large tree completely uprooted unless the magnitude of the hurricane or tornado was of the highest level. Tree roots are firmer than the foundations of a house. This demonstrates that our faith anchors us during times of trial. When the winds of change continuously blow problems our way, what will keep us firm and steady? The Tree of Faith. Without it, we are like leaves, and when calamity strikes, we will be scattered easily by the winds. We will neither have the ability to offer any resistance to the power of the winds nor the ability to remain firm in our place. However, if we have faith, we will be like this beautiful tree: come what may, our faith will anchor us and allow us to overcome the challenge at hand.

The branches of this tree are towering in the sky. It is a soaring majestic tree, a tree of immense beauty and benefit: no worldly creation can hide it from the view of mankind. Similarly, our faith cannot be hidden. It will be demonstrated in all aspects of our life; from how we eat and drink to how we interact with our family. It will be displayed in our manners, our humility and how we choose to live our life. That is why Allah tells us that this tree is towering towards the heavens: it is a visible landmark. It is also uplifting because the Tree of Faith will elevate and direct us towards Paradise, the ultimate goal for all mankind.

Allah says, *"It produces fruits all the time."* Notice He uses the plural 'fruits'. Every other tree on the earth will give us only one type of fruit at one time of the year, but the Tree of Faith is unique in that it will give multiple fruits for the plucking, whatever the season. Fruit nourishes us and similarly, the Tree of Faith sustains us in every situation. If we consume that nourishment we will always feel its strength. If we are feeling depressed or lacking purpose in life, our Tree of Faith needs strengthening. If it is strong, we will be able to pluck its fruits to overcome and find a solution to any problem we are faced within our lives.

What are some of the fruits of this beautiful Tree of Faith? The Quran mentions many, foremost amongst them is the blessing of entry into the highest level of Paradise. Allah tells us, *"Verily! Those who have believed and done righteous deeds, they shall have Jannah al-Firdous as a lodging."* [1] This is because *īmān* (faith) prevents us from falling into major sins. We are all struggling to live good lives, but if we have sincere faith, we will be morally conscious and upright. The way to ensure that we live the best life possible in this temporary world is to wholeheartedly turn to faith and aspire to increase our level of faith as much as possible.

Īmān also protects us from the punishment of Allah and His

1 *al-Kahf* 18: 107

anger. Our Prophet ﷺ told us regarding the Hellfire, *"And whoever said: 'None has the right to be worshipped but Allah and has in his heart good (faith) equal to the weight of a wheat grain will be taken out of Hell."*[2] A person with even a tiny amount of faith in his heart will eventually be removed from the Hellfire. Faith guarantees us Allah's protection. He tells us, *"Allah is the protector of those who have faith..."*[3] If He is protecting us, who can possibly cause us any harm?

One of the blessings from the fruit of *īmān* is that it causes our ranks to be raised both in this world and in the next. Many believers do not realise that Allah promises to bless them with a sweet life in this world. Believers sometimes think it is either a difficult life in this world and a good one in the next or enjoy this life and suffer in the next. It is, however, possible to have a good life in both this world and the life hereafter. Allah tells us explicitly, "*Whoever has faith and does good, male or female, We are going to grant them a sweet life in this world...*" [4] The narrow-mindedness that so many of us are guilty of, is thinking that the sweetness of this life lies solely in wealth. True contentment lies within, not without. When we have faith in Allah, we will find the inner peace that all of mankind is searching for. What we have or do not have will become irrelevant, because we have a treasure that is far more important than anything this world can give. True contentment and satisfaction come from *īmān*.

One of the blessings of *īmān* for the believer is that they are never at a loss. The Prophet ﷺ told us, *"Amazing is the affair of the believer, verily all of his affairs are good, and this is not for anyone except the believer. If something of good or happiness befalls him, he is grateful and that is good for him. If something of harm befalls him,*

---

2 *Ṣaḥīḥ* al-Bukhārī 44

3 *al-Baqarah* 2: 257

4 *an-Naḥl* 16: 97

he is patient and that is good for him." [5] No matter what situation they are in, the true believer will always find relief. Allah says, "... *Whoever truly has consciousness of Allah, Allah will provide a way out for him, and Allah will give him what he wants from a source he never expected."* [6] We learn in the Quran that during the Battle of the Trench, when ten thousand pagans surrounded Madīnah, the hypocrites spread fear and lies amongst the Muslims. Allah said, *"Those to whom the hypocrites said, 'Indeed, the people have gathered against you, so fear them.' But it [merely] increased them in faith, and they said, 'Sufficient for us is Allah, and [He is] the best Disposer of affairs."* [7] During this great trial, the *īmān* of the *Ṣaḥābah* (Companions) increased as opposed to decreased. They turned to Allah sincerely and He took care of them, sending a sandstorm to their aid. Without lifting a sword, the pagans were prevented from entering the city. The believers will never fear because Allah will take care of them, and this is from the fruits and blessings of *īmān.*

The people of faith are promised a beautiful end to the life of this world. Death is inevitable, and for the vast majority of people, this will be the most difficult time of their lives: this is not the case for the believer. Allah tells us, *"Indeed, those who have said, 'Our Lord is Allah,' and then remained on a right course - the angels will descend upon them, [saying], 'Do not fear and do not grieve but receive good tidings of Paradise, which you were promised."* [8] When the believer has one foot in this world and the other in the next, the angels will come down and calm them and their soul will leave their body smoothly, comparable to the ease at which water pours out from a vessel.

There is one blessing of *īmān* that truly outshines all the rest.

---

5 *Ṣaḥīḥ* Muslim 2999
6 *aṭ-Ṭalāq* 65: 2
7 *'Āl 'Imrān* 3: 173
8 *Fuṣṣilat* 41: 30

Allah tells us the believer will have, *"...Al-Husna, and more than Paradise itself..."* [9] *Al-Husna* is one of the names of Paradise, and the Prophet ﷺ told us that this 'more' than Paradise, is the blessing of seeing Allah directly. He said, *"When the people of Paradise enter it, Allah Almighty will say: Would you like anything more? They will say: Have You not brightened our faces? Have You not admitted us into Paradise and saved us from Hellfire? Then, Allah will lift the veil and nothing they are given will be more beloved to them than looking at their Lord Almighty."* [10] The Prophet ﷺ then recited this verse. For the believers to see their Lord is by far the greatest blessing of *īmān.*

Let us reflect for a moment on the concept of *īmān.* We translate it as 'faith' and yet this is not a truly accurate translation: *īmān* is more than solely belief. Many people mistakenly think that simply believing will suffice to earn them these rewards, but all we need to expose this error is to look at the example of Iblīs (Satan) himself. He believes in the existence of Allah, the Day of Judgment and that Allah sends prophets, but Iblīs is not a believer. Iblīs is neither an atheist nor agnostic: he believes, yet he is not a believer. Why? Allah tells us that Iblīs refused to implement the knowledge that he had. When Allah told him to prostrate, he refused. Arrogance is what made Iblīs what he is, not the rejection of belief. If we look in the Quran, Allah never once praises just having faith. It is always, *"Those who believe and do good deeds..."* [11] Belief in combination with good actions goes hand in hand. We need to show our Islam in our actions, to be like this tall tree towering in the sky.

The Tree of Faith is the ultimate life source, giving us the best in this world and the next. If we want to pluck off its fruits, we need to make sure that we give this tree its due. Nurture it with the

9 *Yūnus* 10: 26
10 *Ṣaḥīḥ* Muslim 181
11 *al-Baqarah* 2: 82

sunlight of the Quran and *Sunnah* and nourish it with our actions and good deeds. The more we do this, the bigger our tree will grow. If we allow the weeds of sins to flourish, our tree will not be able to obtain full nourishment. It will wither away and die. Our Tree of Faith is our most valuable possession. It will sustain us through all the trials of this world so we need to make sure that we guard it accordingly and nurture it. Only then will we be able to reap the rewards of this beautiful tree, and all these fruits and blessings of *īmān*.

Journey of Worship

2

Journey of Worship

أَلا بِذِكرِ اللَّهِ تَطمَئِنُّ القُلوبُ

"... Verily, in the remembrance of Allah do hearts find tranquillity."

(*ar-Ra'd* 13: 28)

The most fundamental principle of Islam is that we have been created for a specific and noble purpose: the worship of Allah. Allah tells us, *"I did not create jinn and mankind except to worship Me."* [12] If we were asked 'why do we worship Allah?', the vast majority of us would respond with something along the lines of, 'Because He created me'. However, this concept is fundamentally flawed and a too simplistic way of analysing the question posed. We should worship Allah because of who He is and not because of who we are. Allah tells us in the Quran, *"...unto Him all praise is due, at the beginning and at the end of time..."* [13] He was worthy

12 *adh-Dhāriyāt* 51: 56
13 *al-Qaṣaṣ* 28: 70

of worship before He made the creation, and He will be worthy of being worshipped after it perishes.

The best example that illustrates this point is that of our beloved Prophet Muḥammad ﷺ. No human being was nobler or more perfect a worshipper than him. Yet what would our beloved Prophet Muḥammad ﷺ say in the middle of the night as he prostrated? *"...I cannot fully praise You, for You are as You have praised yourself."*[14] Take a moment to reflect on who is saying this: the most perfect worshipper of Allah. Consider when he is saying this: during the most blessed period, the last third of the night. Consider what state he is in while saying this: the state of prostration, the most submissive state a person can be in. The best man, in the best time, in the best posture, is acknowledging that he is not able to worship Allah as He deserves to be worshipped. If this is the case for him, then how about us? Are we able to fulfil the requirements with all the deficiencies we possess?

Think of the angels. Their sole purpose in life is to execute the commandments of Allah and they worship Him constantly. The Prophet ﷺ said in a beautiful hadith: *"The heaven makes a noise like groaning, and it has the right to, for there is no space in it the width of four fingers, but there is an angel there, standing, or bowing, or placing his forehead in sujūd to Allah."* [15] The angels worship Allah without eating, drinking, sleeping or becoming tired. They were created before ʾĀdam and they shall live long after the destruction of the earth. Yet, how will the angels respond after they face death? *"Glory be to You. We did not worship You as You deserve to be worshipped."* [16] Now, let us assess our scenario. Throughout the lifespan of an average person, in total we worship Allah for a few short years, we stand in total may be an average of twenty minutes a day for

14 *Ṣaḥīḥ* Muslim 486
15 *Sunan* at-Tirmidhī 2312
16 *al-Awsaṭ* ạ-Ṭabarāni 4:44

prayer and yet we think we have accomplished a lot. We need to constantly remind ourselves as well as our fellow brothers and sisters, in a humble manner, that worship of Allah is, in fact, the very purpose of our creation.

How do we worship Allah? Allah is worshipped by a specific set of beliefs, statements and actions that are detailed in the Hadith of Jibrīl. It tells us what we have to believe, what we have to say and what we have to do, to worship Allah correctly. The Prophet ﷺ told his Companions to ask him something about the religion, but they were too shy to ask, therefore Allah, from his Mercy, sent the Angel Jibrīl to ask a series of simple questions. What is Islam? The Prophet ﷺ replied that *"Islam is to testify there is no God but Allah and Muhammad is the Messenger of Allah, to establish prayer, to give charity, to fast the month of Ramaḍān, and to perform pilgrimage to the House if a way is possible."* This was then followed by the question of what is *īmān*? The Prophet ﷺ said, *"Īmān is to believe in Allah, His angels, His books, His messengers, the Last Day, and to believe in providence (qadr), its good and its evil."* Which was then followed by the question of what is *ʾiḥsān* (excellence)? The Prophet ﷺ told us, *"ʾIḥsān is to worship Allah as if you see Him, for if you do not see Him, He surely sees you."*[17] In these few short sentences, the Prophet ﷺ detailed the fundamentals of our religion. Our theology, our *fiqh* (jurisprudence), our *sulūk* (spirituality) and our relationship with Allah all stem from our understanding of this hadith.

How do we perfect our worship? Of the best ways to revive and rejuvenate our spirit, and to saturate ourselves with the servitude of Allah, is to increase our consciousness of Him through knowledge. Nothing brings about enhanced spirituality like knowledge. When a person stands up to pray, the Prophet ﷺ said that it is possible

17 *Ṣaḥīḥ* Muslim 8

that for that person, nothing is written for them. Another person might stand up to pray and receive one-tenth of the reward, the next two tenths, and so on until the tenth person will get the entire reward of the prayer. Outwardly, they are doing the same action. So what makes one of them obtain nothing while another is a recipient of a perfect reward? They are distinguished by the motivation and the religiosity that is present in the heart: the inner spirituality.

Open up any book of hadith and we will read that when the Prophet ﷺ stood up to pray he started with, '*Allāhu Akbar.*' When we stand up to pray after reading that, we will feel a deeper sense of attachment and an understanding of the what the Prophet ﷺ meant when he said, "*...Pray as you have seen me praying...*" [18] There is a science known as *faḍā'il* or 'blessings' and it is different from the *fiqh* and the practice. When we study the blessings of performing *wuḍū'* we learn that the Prophet ﷺ said that every drop of water that touches our skin and falls during the process of fulfilling *wuḍū*, takes a sin with it. As we are reminded of this, it Is an opportunity to reflect on the previous sins we have committed while also being grateful to Allah for the blessing which can be found while performing *wuḍū'*. Knowledge brings consciousness and servitude into our acts of worship.

At this point, I would like to recommend one particular book which I believe will be of benefit for all of us in improving our attachment to our Creator: *Riyāḍ al-Ṣāliḥīn*, 'Gardens of the Righteous' by Imām al-Nawawī. This is truly a blessed book, one that he wrote specifically targetting the mass population of Muslims. In it, he compiles simple hadith, mainly about *faḍā'il*, and offers us the ability to read about and appreciate the blessings of any action. When we understand more deeply the significance behind these actions, it creates a connection between us and

18 *Ṣaḥīḥ* al-Bukhārī 631

the texts — the Quran and the *Sunnah* — and automatically our spirituality and our servitude will increase. The irony is we are all doing the same actions, but just an ounce of knowledge can give us the spirituality that we are lacking in our lives. It is of paramount importance that we make it a constant part of our daily routine, a few minutes with the Quran and a few minutes with the *Sunnah.*

What are the levels of worship? The Hadith of Jibrīl shows us that there are three levels of worship: Islam, īmān and *ʾiḥsān.* They correspond to the three categories of believers: the Muslim, the *muʾmin* and the *muḥsin.* What makes a person a Muslim versus a *muʾmin* or a *muḥsin* and what are the things that take us from one level to the next?

A Muslim is one who performs the minimum required by our religion: the five pillars of Islam. A Bedouin once came to the Prophet ﷺ and said, "Tell me of a deed such that if I were to do it, I would enter Paradise." The Prophet ﷺ said, *"Worship Allah without worshipping anything along with Him, offer the prescribed prayers, pay the compulsory charity, and fast the month of Ramaḍān."* The Bedouin said, "I swear by Him in whose hands my life is, I will not do more than this." When the Bedouin left, the Prophet ﷺ said, *"Whoever would like to see a man of Paradise should look at this man."* [19] The Companions were shocked because they thought what this man was doing was nothing significant. The Prophet ﷺ told them that if he was able to fulfil these basic conditions, he would pass the test. Look at how times have changed! How many of us today even reach this basic level of fulfilling the five pillars of Islam?

A higher level is to be a *muʾmin* or one who has īmān. Every single deed has that which is obligatory, that which is *Sunnah,* which the Prophet ﷺ would do regularly, and that which is *nafl,*

19 *Ṣaḥīḥ* al-Bukhārī 1397

which he would do occasionally. The scholars have defined the level of the *mu'min* as being one who does the bare minimum, plus the *Sunnah* and occasional *nafl* actions. The *mu'min* reaches a higher level primarily through the overall quantity of their actions: they do more than the Muslim. Added to this, the *mu'min* will avoid sins, in particular the major sins.

What makes a person rise from the level of īmān to that of *'iḥsān*? This is a crucial question, from which we can learn how to improve as Muslims. How did the Prophet ﷺ define the *muḥsin*, the one who has reached the level of *'iḥsān*? He ﷺ said that they worship Allah as though they see Him. In other words, they are aware that Allah sees them at all times and are therefore constantly worshipping Him. This shows us that the *muḥsin* reaches almost the level of the angels in terms of worship, but how? Does the *muḥsin* cut away from society, live in a cave, pray *tahajjud* (night prayer) every night? Was this the way of our beloved Prophet ﷺ, or the Companions, or the famous *imāms*? The answer is a resounding 'no'. They worshipped Allah and they lived like human beings and yet they reached the level of *'iḥsān*. So how do we reach this level?

What separates the *mu'min* from the *muḥsin* is something that many people at present do not completely understand. For the *mu'min*, there is a clear division between the religious and worldly life. They go to work or about their daily activities and when the prescribed time of prayers arrives, they pray the prayer with the *Sunnah*, they make *dhikr* and *du'ā'* and then go back to continue with the activity they were partaking in previously. Internally, they have a secular life and a sacred one. It is a dichotomy, a two-vision view of the world. The *muḥsin* transcends this division and for them everything becomes religious. They are always thinking of Allah, appreciating the fact that He is watching over them. The beauty of Islam is that once we reach the required quantity of deeds, it is the inward spiritual quality that determines our level, and therefore our reward.

One of the most beautiful incidents that demonstrates this point comes from Muʿādh ibn Jabal, may Allah be pleased with him. He was staying with some friends and they asked him to describe his *tahajjud* prayer. Look at the topic of conversation! For the Companions, the first question on their mind was the topic of how they could become better Muslims. He explained to them that he slept for a certain period, stood in prayer and then lay down again before *fajr.* He concluded by saying that he expected to be rewarded for his sleep, just as much as he expected to be rewarded for his prayer. Think about that for a moment. It was not that Muʿādh spent eight hours praying with no sleep. He had a healthy night's sleep, but he also prayed, and he had this matter of fact understanding that he would be rewarded for both. This is what you call the level of *ʾiḥsān.*

By deepening our knowledge, understanding and awareness, the concept of worship branches out to encompass every aspect of our lives. We can be rewarded for mundane acts just as we are rewarded for the prayer, because of our level of consciousness of Allah. This concept is illustrated in the statement of one of the *Tābiʿūn,* Bakr al-Muzannī (d. 108 AH), when he said, *"Abū Bakr did not precede you because of more fasts, prayer and dhikr, but because of something that came into his heart and settled in his consciousness."* [20] Obtaining and achieving the correct level of spirituality is what elevates us on this journey of worship.

---

20 *Nawādir al-Uṣūl fī Maʿrifat Aḥādīth al-Rasūl* Ḥakīm at-Tirmidhī 1/148

Prayer

3

Prayer

رَبِّ اجعَلني مُقيمَ الصَّلاةِ

"My Lord, make me an establisher of the prayer..."

(*Ibrāhīm* 14: 40)

Even for the best amongst us, there are times in life when the prayer can become monotonous and routine. That is why persevering and maintaining one's concentration in *ṣalāh* is one of the highest signs of īmān. The ultimate goal of our prayer extends beyond carrying out the motions; it is the spirituality behind the actions. Allah tells us, *"Certainly will the believer have succeeded: they who are, during their prayer, humbly submissive."*[21] Being 'humbly submissive', or having *khushū*, is to simultaneously have an element of both hope and fear in our heart, as well as the consciousness of Allah and submission to Him.

There are three separate incidents mentioned in the Quran that show us the importance of the prayer. The first of these occurred

21 *al-Mu'minūn* 23: 1-2

when Allah showed Prophet Mūsā (Moses), peace be upon him, the Burning Bush. Mūsā was still a shepherd in Madian at the time, wondering in the valley and he did not know that he was a prophet or what was about to happen to him. Allah called him to *Ṭūr Sīnā* (Mount Sanai) and spoke to him directly. This was the first time that Mūsā was receiving Revelation. What was the message? *"Indeed I am Allah. There is no deity except Me, so worship Me."* The question which arises after this statement, is how does one worship? *"Establish the prayer for My remembrance."*[22]

The second example is that of our beloved Prophet Muḥammad ﷺ. There was only one time in his life when so important was the message, he ﷺ was called into the presence of Allah. No other commandment in our religion was revealed in this way. We know that Jibrīl accompanied the Prophet ﷺ up through the heavens until Jibrīl reached the stage beyond which he did not have permission to go any higher, instructing the Prophet ﷺ to continue alone from there. The Prophet ﷺ rose to such heights that he could hear the pen writing in *Al-Lawh al-Mahfūdh* (The Preserved Tablet). He rose to the highest level that any human being has ever travelled to receive Revelation directly from Allah. What was the Message? *Establish the prayer.*

We know that the initial commandment was to pray fifty times a day. Allah willed that the Prophet ﷺ travel back down until he met the Prophet Mūsā, peace be upon him, who had lived for more than 130 years. He had decades more experience and his people had tested him in ways different from the way our *ummah* tested the Prophet Muḥammad. Mūsā said, *"Return to your Lord and beg for a reduction [in the number of prayers], for your community shall not be able to bear this burden. I have put to test the Children of Israel and tried them [and found them too weak to bear such a heavy*

---

22 *Ṭā' Hā'* 20: 14

burden]."[23] The Prophet ﷺ returned to the presence of Allah and the prayer was eventually reduced to five times a day. The question arises: surely Allah already knew that the prayer would be legislated at five times a day. Of course, Allah knew, so why go through the process of reducing it? There are two pearls of wisdom that we can find from this story. The first we learn in hadith. After the Prophet had gone back and forth and the number of prayers had been reduced to five, Allah said, *"These five prayers will be recorded for you as fifty [in reward]."*[24] This is the first wisdom: we will pray five prayers a day but get the reward of praying fifty times a day. The second wisdom is a spiritual message. If Allah had legislated the prayer of fifty times a day, it would take nearly all of our time throughout the day. This shows us that prayer is the only reason we exist. The very purpose of our creation is to fulfil the commandment of prayer. Our Lord spoke to the Prophet Mūsā and called him to *Ṭur Sīnā,* and He spoke to the Prophet Muḥammad and called him into His Divine presence, to show us that the importance of prayer outweighs everything else.

The third case that illustrates its importance is the father of both of these men, the Prophet Ibrāhīm (Abraham), peace be upon him. Prayer was intrinsically linked to his building of the House of Allah, the *Kaʿbah.* Allah tells us, *"Indeed, the first House [of worship] established for mankind was that at Makkah..."*[25] Allah honours the *Kaʿbah* by ascribing it to Himself, calling it *"...My House..."*[26] Anything that Allah ascribes to Himself in ownership becomes sacred and blessed. Allah told the Prophet Ibrāhīm, *"... Do not associate anything with Me and purify My House for those who perform Ṭawāf and those who stand [in prayer] and those who*

23 *Ṣaḥīḥ* Muslim 309
24 *Sunan* at-Tirmidhī 213
25 *'Āl 'Imrān* 3: 96
26 *al-Baqarah* 2: 125

bow and prostrate."[27] So important is the prayer that it was linked directly to the *Ka'bah*. That is why, when it was being built, the *du'ā'* on the tongue of Ibrāhīm was, *"My Lord, make me an establisher of prayer, and [many] from my descendants..."*[28] Notice the words '*establisher of the prayer*'. The Quran never refers to just 'praying', it's: 'establish the prayer', 'perfect the prayer' and 'rectify the prayer'. The criteria of prayer are not merely about offering the rituals; it's *perfecting* the actions of the body and the heart.

For every single Prophet, you can find references to the importance of the prayer. Think of the Prophet 'Īsā (Jesus), peace be upon him when Maryam came back to the city after giving birth and Allah had forbidden her to speak. The people surrounded her accusingly, so Maryam pointed to the sky and pointed at the baby. Allah then initiated baby 'Īsā to speak. What did he say? *"Indeed, I am a servant of Allah. He has given me the Scripture and made me a Prophet. And He has blessed me wherever I am and has enjoined upon me prayer and zakāh as long as I live."*[29] The first *khuṭbah* of 'Īsā as a day-old baby was, 'Allah has commanded me to pray.'

Look at the extraordinary status of the prayer. There is no greater deed on the face of this earth that we can do: no other form of worship that is more blessed. When the Prophet ﷺ was asked, 'Which deed is the dearest to Allah?', he replied, *"To offer the prayers at their early stated fixed times."*[30] Establishing the prayer is the most beloved thing that we can do in the sight of Allah and it is the key to our success in this world and the next.

27 *al-Hajj* 22: 26
28 *Ibrāhīm* 14: 40
29 *Maryam* 19: 30-31
30 *Ṣaḥīḥ* al-Bukhārī 527

Quran

4

Quran

وَهَٰذَا ذِكْرٌ مُّبَارَكٌ أَنزَلْنَاهُ ۚ أَفَأَنتُمْ لَهُ مُنكِرُونَ

"And this is a blessed Reminder which We have sent down, will you then deny it?"

(al-'Anbiyā' 21: 50)

When somebody asks us how we know that Islam is the true religion, we usually respond by saying that the Quran is a miracle, but very few of us truly understand why. What makes the Quran miraculous? The Prophet ﷺ said, *"There is no Prophet amongst the prophets but was given miracles of which people had security or had belief, but what I was given was Divine Inspiration which Allah revealed to me. So I hope that my followers will be more than those of any other Prophet on the Day of Resurrection."*[31] Every Prophet was given a miracle that resulted in the people during that period to believe. The Prophet ﷺ told us that his miracle was the

31 *Ṣaḥīḥ* al-Bukhārī 7274

waḥy, the inspiration that Allah revealed to him, and that because of it he hoped to have the largest number of followers of the Day of Judgment. The Quran was not the Prophet's only miracle; he had multiple miracles ascribed to him throughout his life. However, he wanted to emphasise that the quality of the miracle of the Quran is so powerful that all other miracles become insignificant in comparison to the miracle of the Quran.

Let us compare the miracle of the Quran revealed to Prophet ﷺ, to the miracles of some of the other Prophets. The Prophet Sulaymān (Solomon), peace be upon him, was given power over the wind and the *jinn* and the ability to speak to animals. Prophet Mūsā, peace be upon him, split the Red Sea and Prophet ʿĪsā, peace be upon him, healed the sick and resurrected the dead. Why is the Quran more powerful than any of these miracles?

There are two reasons. The first is the time-space factor. Every other miracle took place in front of a select group of people who were the only ones to have witnessed it. We as present-day Muslims firmly believe that such events did occur historically because Allah says that they happened, although we were not there to witness the event. What about the Quran? Do we have to have been in 7th century Arabia to witness the miracle of the Quran, to recite it or experience it? No. The time-space factor has been eliminated. The Quran is the only miracle that we can literally feel and experience the impact of directly. We have the same access to the Book of Allah as any generation before us had. The Quran is an eternal living miracle.

The second reason why the miracle of the Quran is more powerful than any other miracle is that it does not require external supporting evidence. Every other Book of Allah had miracles revealed with it to prove that the Book was from Him. The Prophet ʿĪsā came with the *Injīl* (New Testament) and miracles to prove that it was a Book from Allah, and the Prophet Mūsā came with the *Torah* (Old Testament), and its associated miracles. What about the Quran? What is the miracle that proves that the Quran is a revelation from Allah? The Quran itself is the miracle. It does not need external supporting evidence to prove its claim that it is the Book of Allah. It is the evidence and the Message combined in one. No other prophet was given such a miracle through his Book. That is why the Prophet ﷺ said that because of the Quran, he hoped to have the largest number of followers on the Day of Judgment. The miracle of the Quran is so powerful that it will cause large numbers of people to believe.

To fully comprehend how the Quran is a miraculous book, we need to look at the 'Verses of Challenge'. These verses were revealed one after another over approximately fifteen years and each of them issues a different challenge to the people of the time to try and produce something comparable to the Quran. The earliest verse is the strongest, *"...If mankind and the jinn gathered in order to produce the like of this Quran, they could not produce the like of it..."*[32] When they failed to do that Allah told them to try ten verses. When they couldn't do that He reduced it until He issued the final verse of the challenge, *"And if you are in doubt about what has been sent down upon our servant [Muhammad], then produce a Sūrah the like thereof and call upon your witnesses other than Allah, if you should be truthful."*[33] Allah then sealed the challenge, *"But if you do not — and you will never be able to — then fear the Fire, whose fuel is men and stones, prepared for the disbelievers."*[34] Within the miracle is another miracle, the prediction that the Quran will never be replicated or beaten. If you are not able to bring a verse like it then be prepared to meet the punishment of Allah: this is a simple and powerful statement directed to mankind. The miracle and the

32 *al-'Isrā'* 17: 88
33 *al-Baqarah* 2: 23
34 *al-Baqarah* 2: 24

challenge of the Quran has now been effectively sealed. The final ultimatum has been given.

So the question is, what would someone have to do to bring a similar Quran? What conditions would have to be met? There are at least twenty points that the leading scholars of the present and past have identified, but here I will outline just a few. Firstly, and the most obvious for those who know the Quran in its native language, is the sheer power and eloquence of the Arabic of the Quran. This was what the Arabs immediately felt when they listened to it. They had mastered all types of rhetoric and linguistic devices and they even had an entire discipline of different types of poetry. The Quran came and it was simply unclassifiable. It became a new genre due to its unique rhythm and its distinctive rhyme. There was nothing that could compare nor compete with the style of the Quran, in its syntax and concise and detailed nature.

The second point that proves the miraculous nature of the Quran is its predictions. There is no denying that the Quran has many predictions in it, but perhaps the most obvious and the most amazing is the prediction that the Quran itself will remain uncorrupted, preserved and unchallenged until the end of time. Allah tells us, *"Indeed, it is We who sent down the Quran and indeed, We will be its Guardian."*[35] To this day, the Muslim *ummah* has never disagreed about the content of their Holy Book. Every other religion has disagreements about the content of their Book. Muslims do not realise how they have been blessed with certainty in regards to the preserved nature of the Quran.

The third unique feature is the stories contained within the Quran. Multiple times, when Allah mentions the story of a previous Prophet, He follows it up with an interesting verse. For example, Allah mentions the story of the Prophet Mūsā on *Ṭūr Sīnā*

35 *al- Ḥijr* 15: 9

and then says to the Prophet ﷺ *"And you were not on the western side [of the mount] when we revealed to Mūsā the command, and you were not among the witnesses [to that]."*[36] What is the purpose of saying, 'you were not there'? Allah is saying, 'how else did you get this information'? Our Prophet ﷺ was told in the Quran, *"This is from the news of the unseen which We reveal to you, You knew it not, neither you nor your people, before this..."*[37] In the age of the internet and libraries, it is difficult for us to understand why this is a miracle, but to put this into present time context, it is like an isolated tribe in the Brazilian rainforest, who has had no contact with the outside world and no access to modern-day technology, suddenly knowing the history of the European kings.

The fourth miracle is the theology of the Quran, the content of the message in terms of belief and laws: the *Sharīʿah*. This is not one point but numerous points in one. Of the miracles of the Quran is what it preaches and teaches. This includes morality, theology, monotheism, the perfection of Allah's Names and Attributes and detailed laws of inheritance, amongst other things. These were laws perfectly suited to humanity, bringing about peace and justice. They came from the Prophet ﷺ who did not have any formal education comparable to that of the present day, who was an illiterate shepherd in the desert, and through them, the Prophet ﷺ became a mercy to all of mankind.

The fifth point is one of the more popular aspects of our current times: scientific miracles. There are many books written about the scientific miracles of the Quran and these are undeniably true. The Quran uses terminologies and descriptions that are beyond anything anyone from the 7th century in Makkah would have known. That Allah says, *"...all [heavenly bodies] in an orbit*

---

36 *al-Qaṣaṣ* 28: 44
37 *Hūd* 11: 49

swimming"[38] at a time when no one thought that the earth moved, or that the embryo is described as coming from the mixing of male and female fluids are no doubt from the scientific miracles of the Quran. However, we need to take this miraculous aspect with some caution. The Quran is not a book of science: it is a book of guidance. In parts of that guidance, Allah uses terminology that shows that it is applicable beyond the period during which it was revealed to the Prophet ﷺ. In my opinion, the miracle of the Quran is that the language accommodates what we now know of science, not that it predicts science, and there is a difference between the two.

The sixth of the miracles of the Quran is the effect it has on its listeners. Even non-Muslims find the Quran beautiful to listen to without knowing what it means. Muslims who do not understand Arabic or the meaning of the words are moved by the sound of the recitation, and for those who do understand, the message is even more profound. Allah says, *"And when they hear what has been revealed to the Messenger, you see their eyes overflowing with tears because of what they have recognised of the Truth..."*[39]

The final point that I want to mention is the way the Quran is memorised. It can be remembered and recited with an ease that is impossible for any other book. Allah says, *"The Quran is distinct verses [preserved] within the breasts of those who have been given knowledge..."*[40] No other religious tradition memorises its book of scripture in totality. As Muslims, we do not just have just one or two people memorising the Quran: every single community of Muslims around the world has people who have memorised the complete content of the Quran. A *ḥāfidth* is a living, walking, talking miraculous sign that the Quran is the preserved Book of

38 *al-'Anbiyā'* 21: 33
39 *al-Mā'idah* 5: 83
40 *al-'Ankabūt* 29: 49

Allah. What other book is there, at six hundred pages long with more than six thousand verses that can be memorised, typically in a language unknown to the memoriser? A ten-year old child who does not even know one word of Arabic can recite the entire book from memory as if they are reciting it straight from the page. Is this not in itself a miracle? This is one of the most tangible pieces of evidence of this Book being from Allah.

Much more can be said about the miracle of the Quran, and the list I have provided here is only limited, but as Muslims, we do not need a list to tell us that the Quran is a miracle. We know and have come to accept it is a miracle when we listen to it. We feel it is a miracle when we experience it. We appreciate the miracle when we are immersed in its recitation and understanding its meanings. Because it is the speech of Allah, it has all of these miraculous qualities and amazing things associated with it. When the Quran is His speech, it will be nothing like our speech and we will appreciate and recognise that in every single word that we recite.

Love of the Prophet

5
Love of the Prophet

لَقَد كَانَ لَكُم فِي رَسولِ اللَّهِ أُسوَةٌ حَسَنَةٌ لِمَن كَانَ
يَرجُو اللَّهَ وَاليَومَ الآخِرَ وَذَكَرَ اللَّهَ كَثيرًا

"Indeed in the Messenger of Allah,
you have a good example to follow,
for him who hopes in (the Meeting with) Allah,
and the Last Day,
and remembers Allah much."

(*al-'Aḥzāb* 33: 21)

Imām al-Qasṭallānī (d. 923 AH), in his magnum opus on the life and times of the Prophet Muḥammad ﷺ wrote:

"Remember that the love of the Prophet is the highest level of faith for which believers compete with one another against; and for it, workers of good deeds aim; and within it, all other love dissolves... And if a person begins to love someone who is kind to him once or twice or a few times, a kindness that is temporary,

or saves him from a calamity that itself would not have lasted, then how much more should one love he who has gifted him with an eternal gift (of Paradise), and who has saved him through his teachings from eternal punishment? And if a person begins to love someone who has a good characteristic or two, or has a good appearance, then how much more should one love he who has perfected all good characteristics and he who is more handsome than the full moon...?"[41]

To taste the sweetness of faith, Allah and His Messenger must be dearer to us than anything else. The Prophet ﷺ said, *"None of you will have faith till he loves me more than his father, his children and all mankind."*[42] We see this illustrated in the narration of ʿAbdullāh bin Hisham who said, "We were with the Prophet and he was holding the hand of ʿUmar ibn al-Khaṭṭāb. ʿUmar said to him, "O Allah's Messenger! You are dearer to me than everything except my own self." The Prophet said, *"No, by Him in Whose Hand my soul is, (you will not have complete faith) till I am dearer to you than your own self."*[43]

We cannot imagine a Muslim, in whichever land they live, saying that they believe in Allah without loving the Prophet ﷺ. Yet despite this fact, when we look at the Muslim community as a whole, we find that something has gone very wrong. We say that we love the Prophet ﷺ with our tongues and our lips, yet our daily actions do not reflect this. Many of us do not even know ten hadith or ten incidents from the *Sīrah*. We have neglected to study the Prophet's life and most of us remain ignorant of his excellent example. Thus, we find ourselves far from actually having the true love of the Prophet ﷺ.

41 *al-Mūwāhib al-Lādunniyya* al-Qasṭallānī
42 *Ṣaḥīḥ* al-Bukhārī 15
43 *Ṣaḥīḥ* al-Bukhārī 6632

The primary way to increase our love of the Prophet ﷺ is to learn about his life. Allah tells us in the Quran, *"Each [story] We relate to you from the news of the Messengers is that by which We make firm your heart..."*[44] The stories of the Prophets of old strengthened our Prophet's faith and in the same way, studying his *Sīrah* will strengthen our faith. It will deepen our love for the Prophet ﷺ and when we love him, we will want to know everything about him and imitate him in every way possible.

The word *Sīrah* means 'to traverse or to journey', and it is derived from the root word meaning 'to travel'. The reason why it is called the *Sīrah,* is because you are travelling his journey and following in his footsteps. Allah tells us in the Quran, *"Indeed in the Messenger of Allah you have a good example to follow for him who hopes in (the Meeting with) Allah and the Last Day and remembers Allah much."*[45] Studying the *Sīrah* and how the Prophet ﷺ lived his life will show us the best way to live our own lives. It will show us how to worship Allah, how to have the best morals and manners and how to be the best leader. It will also provide us with the best model for achieving success within our family and community life. It is from the perfection of Allah's wisdom that He sent the Prophet ﷺ as a human being in flesh and blood, to provide us with the best of all role models.

Studying the Prophet's *Sīrah* reinforces our faith by deepening our understanding of the miracle that was his life. He came from the darkest depths of pagan Arabia, bringing forth the elegance of the Quran and a model for society, leadership and military success. Within fifty years Islam had spread and within one hundred years it ruled the world. This is truly a miracle and the *Sīrah* is the story of that miracle. The Prophet ﷺ wielded such immense power, yet he lived his life in utter simplicity. Ibn Ḥazm (d. 456 AH), the

44 *Hūd* 11: 120
45 *al-'Aḥzāb* 33: 21

famous Andalusian scholar said that if the Prophet ﷺ had not been given any miracle other than his life and times, it would have been sufficient to prove that he was a Prophet of Allah. This is why the *Ṣaḥābah* used to study the *Sīrah* together with the Quran. We should do the same, for both ourselves and our children.

Some of the beautiful characteristics that our Prophet ﷺ embodied were gentleness, patience, generosity, love and care. Anas ibn Mālik served him for ten years and not once did the Prophet ﷺ get angry with him, such was his gentleness and patience. As for his generosity, the Prophet ﷺ was the most charitable and the most generous of all of mankind and he would never refuse anyone who asked anything of him. It is narrated that once the Prophet was wearing a garment that had holes in it and one of the *Ṣaḥābah* gave him a beautiful garment to replace it with. When the Prophet ﷺ put it on another *Companion* asked if he could have it. The Prophet ﷺ agreed and he *immediately* went back home and came back wearing the tattered garment. The Prophet ﷺ generosity was such that when he passed away, he had only seven dirhams to his name.

It was for our Prophet ﷺ that Allah revealed from above the seven heavens, *"And indeed you [O Muḥammad] are of a great moral character."*[46] The more we study the Prophet's *Sīrah*, the more we understand his noble character and our love for him increases. During the Battle of Uhud, when the Prophet ﷺ was injured and his tooth fell out, he said, *"O Allah, forgive my people for they do not know."*[47] During the time of his injury, he was worried as to how Allah would forgive the people who had harmed him. During the Year of Sorrow, when he visited the people in Ṭā'if to give them the message of Islam, the leaders ridiculed him and ordered the children to throw stones at him to such an extent that he bled until his sandals filled with blood. Allah sent the Angel Jibrīl with the

---

46 *al-Qalam* 68: 4
47 *Ṣaḥīḥ* Ibn Ḥibbān 985

Angel of the mountains, offering to crush those who made him bleed if he wished. What did the Prophet say? *"No, but I hope that Allah will let them beget children who will worship Allah alone."*[48] Look at his mercy: because of it, Ṭā'if is now a city populated by Muslims.

The Prophet Muḥammad ﷺ embodied humility and modesty and he lived a very simple lifestyle. It was said that any child or old lady of Madīnah could come to the Prophet and take him by the hand to help in their manual labour, and he would do it, such was his humility. During the Battle of Badr, when three people had to share one camel, he insisted on walking whilst others rode, saying that he was no less in need of Allah's reward. When 'Umar entered upon the Prophet ﷺ house in his small room with no furniture except for a coarse mat made out of date palm fibre, 'Umar began to cry, lamenting that the leaders of Rome and Persia had so much more. The Prophet ﷺ said, *"Won't you be satisfied that they enjoy this world and we the Hereafter?"*[49] This was the life of our beloved Prophet. How does it compare to ours?

As for his love for this *ummah*, Allah says, *"...Grievous to him is what you suffer; [he is] concerned over you and to the believers is kind and merciful."*[50] The Prophet ﷺ told us that every Prophet was granted acceptance of one *du'ā'* and they used it during their life in this world. In his mercy, the Prophet saved his *du'ā'* for us, *"...I wish, if Allah wills, to keep that invocation as intercession for my followers on the Day of Resurrection."*[51] His one *du'ā'*, and he saved it for us so that Allah may forgive us for our sins. Can there be a greater sacrifice than this? This should foster a sense of profound love for him in our hearts.

---

48 *Ṣaḥīḥ* al-Bukhārī 454
49 *Ṣaḥīḥ* al-Bukhārī 4913
50 *at-Tawbah* 9: 128
51 *Ṣaḥīḥ* al-Bukhārī 7474

To love the Prophet ﷺ is one of the requirements of our faith, but what does it mean to love him? What is the condition of this love? Allah tells us in the Quran, *"Say, [O Muḥammad], "If you should truly love Allah, then follow me, [so] Allah will love you and forgive you your sins."*[52] This is called the 'Verse of the Test' because it tests whether or not we love Allah. If we love Allah, then we should love His Messenger and follow his *Sunnah*, and consequently, Allah will love us.

What are the rewards for this love? A Bedouin came to the Prophet ﷺ asking him about the time of the Day of Judgment. The Prophet said, *"It will surely come to pass. What have you prepared for it?"* The man said, "O Messenger of Allah, I have not prepared much in the way of prayer and good works, but I love Allah and His Messenger." The Prophet said, *"You will be with those you love."*[53]

52 *'Āl 'Imrān* 3: 31
53 *Ṣaḥīḥ* al-Bukhārī 688

Born Muslim

6
Born Muslim

الحَمدُ لِلَّهِ الَّذي هَدانا لِهٰذا وَما كُنّا لِنَهتَدِيَ لَولا أَن هَدانَا اللَّهُ

"...Praise to Allah, who has guided us to this; and we would never have been guided if Allah had not guided us..."

(*al-'A'rāf* 7: 43)

The vast majority of us were blessed enough to be born into Muslim families. Our parents took us to the *masjid* as children, and they arranged for us to learn the Quran. Have we ever wondered though, if we had not been born into a Muslim family, would we have discovered Islam? Most of us have never thought about this question. We take Islam for granted, and what we take for granted, by and large, we do not appreciate. But what if we were born into a different religion or civilisation? Would our intellectual curiosity have been strong enough for us to question? Would our conviction for Islam have been deep enough that we would have stood up against our relatives? Would we have been curious enough or courageous enough to go against what our society and culture had taught us if we knew that Truth lay elsewhere?

The Prophet ﷺ told us that those who embrace Islam will receive, "*…a double reward.*"[54] They are given this reward because they have had to change their whole lives for their faith. We can only ask ourselves if we would have had the courage to do the same. Allah tells us in the Quran, "*Say: In the bounty of Allah and in His Mercy - in that let them rejoice; it is better than what they accumulate.*"[55] Ibn Abbās, may Allah be pleased with him, said that the bounty of Allah is Islam and the Mercy of Allah is the Quran. Allah tells us that we should be happy that He blessed us with Islam and that He gifted us with the Quran and that this is greater than any other happiness we can gather.

Do we genuinely have happiness for Islam? We need to understand and appreciate the blessings and gifts that Allah has given us. "*So whoever Allah wants to guide — He expands his breast to [contain] Islam; and whoever He wants to misguide — He makes his breast tight and constricted as though he were climbing into the sky...*"[56] It is Allah's *qadr* (Decree) that I was born into a Muslim family; and it is His *qadr* that my neighbour was not. Islam is a gift that Allah has given me and the least that I can do is appreciate that gift. Not to do so is a type of rejection of the generosity of the One who bestowed us with Islam. Allah reminds us in the Quran about the hypocrites who walked into the *masjid* puffed up with pride, trying to show the favour they were doing to the Prophet ﷺ and Islam. He says, "*They consider it a favour to you that they have accepted Islam. Say, 'Do not consider your Islam a favour to me.*

54 *Ṣaḥīḥ* al-Bukhārī 97
55 *Yūnus* 10: 58
56 *al-'An'ām* 6: 125

Rather, Allah has conferred favour upon you that He has guided you to the faith, if you should be truthful."[57]

Our Prophet ﷺ was reminded, *"You do not guide whom you like, but Allah guides whom He wills..."*[58] Have you ever thought about how much he wanted his uncle Abu Talib's guidance? Yet he was never blessed with it. During the preparations for the Battle of the Trench, the *Ṣaḥābah* were reflecting as they were digging, and they began to recite poetry. The Prophet ﷺ entered the trench and began to recite that poetry with them. What was it? *"O Allah! Were it not for You, We would not have been guided, Nor would we have given in charity, nor prayed."*[59] Just look at the *Ṣaḥābah*! An army of ten thousand men surrounded them, but they were happy because their spirits had Islam.

On a trip to Palestine, I visited *Masjid al-Aqṣā* and I want to share some of the most amazing convert stories I heard there. It is estimated that at least a thousand Israeli's have converted to Islam. This has to be done secretly and the majority of them are silent about their faith. A few have gone public and have had to flee their families as a result. They were all guided to Islam through their own questioning and research and they began contacting Muslims until finally, a small group of brothers came together to give them *da'wah* in Hebrew. They were Israeli Jews who had converted to Islam and each of their stories is very powerful.

One of the women was born into a Jewish family in a Western country and had migrated to Israel for religious reasons. As time went by, she grew agnostic and began looking for Truth elsewhere. She looked into Christianity, Buddhism and other traditions, and in the end, out of desperation, she picked up a Quran. She did not

---

57 *al-Ḥujurāt* 49: 17
58 *al-Qaṣaṣ* 28: 56
59 *Ṣaḥīḥ* al-Bukhārī 4106

think she would find anything in it, because she had always been taught that it was a book full of hatred. She said, 'I read it and read it and read it and I found nothing but peace.' She came across my lectures online and contacted me with her questions. When I travelled to Palestine, we met with her and she gave her *shahādah* in *Masjid al-Aqṣā*. Sadly, she cannot be public about her faith because it will cause issues for her and her family, but she is active in the online *daʿwah* community anonymously.

There was a young woman who had contacted the individuals involved in *daʿwah* when she was sixteen years old saying, 'I have decided to convert.' They wrote back saying they could not do anything because she was a minor. She kept emailing them questions and began to pray in her own house, in the closet. Eventually, the night she turned eighteen, she packed her bags and went to a phone booth to call and say she could not live with her family anymore. The brothers were very worried about the situation, wondering if it was a trap. They went with a group of families, and they spoke to her and found her situation to be genuine. A family who lived outside of Jerusalem, at great risk to themselves, agreed to take her in. In Israel, when you turn eighteen you have to do military service, and her papers came. No-one could do anything because it was an issue between her and her government. She took her paperwork and went to the IDF office wearing her *ḥijāb* and told them she had converted to Islam. For three months her case went back and forth until finally, they excused her. The courage she had to fearlessly be who she was, is truly astounding.

The third story was very emotional for me and I had to hold back my tears. There were brothers and sisters in the group, but as usual, it was more sisters who convert, even in that society. There was one very quiet sister. She did not say a single word other than *salām*. We went around the table with each person telling their story and when it came to her turn she could not speak English. She was a third-generation Israeli who spoke only Hebrew. When her story was translated it was so traumatic I almost cried. She was in her thirties and she was the wife of a Rabbi. After reading on her own and studying Islam, she decided to convert. When her husband found out, he divorced her, threatened her, and then took her to court, saying she was mentally insane and should cease contact with their three children. She had not seen her children for three years because her husband said she was a danger to them because she had embraced Islam. She said to me, 'I swear, if they threw me in jail, I would not give up Islam.' I almost broke down. Here was a woman who did not lie, she did not hide her faith and because of that, they took her children away. She gave up her children for Islam. And what of us? We cannot even give up our sins for Islam.

It makes us think of the experiences of the *Ṣaḥābah* like Bilal ibn Abi Rabaḥ who were persecuted for their faith. We have lost that level of *īmān* in our Muslim societies. These people live in the very land of persecution. They know that their families will view them as traitors, yet they still convert. They have left their society, with nowhere to go, they are giving up their luxury, their life, and in this case their children, for the sake of Allah. If that is not going to cause us to appreciate the blessings we take for granted, then what will?

We learn in the Quran that when people enter *Jannah*, they will say, "*...Praise to Allah, who has guided us to this; and we would never have been guided if Allah had not guided us...*"[60] Our beloved Prophet Muḥammad ﷺ was reminded, "*...You did not know what is the Book or [what is] faith, but We have made it a light by which We guide whom We will of Our servants...*"[61] Even the Messenger

60 *al-A'rāf* 7: 43
61 *ash-Shūrā* 42: 52

of Allah was reminded about the blessings of faith. Let us never forget about the blessings of Islam and the responsibility that comes with that. Allah explicitly tells us, "*...And if you turn away, He will replace you with another people; then they will not be the likes of you.*"[62] The purpose of this gift is to be blessed by it, to act upon it, to love Allah for it and to worship Him. One of the ways that we can thank Allah for this gift is to embody the teachings of Islam and to want others to be guided by it. Each one of us should become a role model for our families, our colleagues, our neighbours and those around us.

Our beloved Prophet ﷺ would make *duʿāʾ* to Allah, "*O Allah, protect me with Islam while standing, protect me with Islam while sitting, protect me with Islam while lying down.*"[63] He always remembered that he was a Muslim because Allah had blessed him with Islam, so he asked Allah to protect him and guide him. This is a prophetic *duʿāʾ*. Let us memorise it, and appreciate the blessing of Islam through it, and let us never take Islam for granted.

62 *Muḥammad* 47: 38
63 *al-Daʿawāt al-Kabīr* Bayhaqī 212

Hard Hearts

7
Hard Hearts

أَلَمْ يَأْنِ لِلَّذِينَ آمَنُوا أَن تَخْشَعَ قُلُوبُهُمْ لِذِكْرِ اللَّهِ
وَمَا نَزَلَ مِنَ الْحَقِّ

"Has the time not come
for those who have believed,
that their hearts should become humbly submissive
at the remembrance of Allah,
and what has come down of the Truth?..."

(*al-Ḥadīd* 57: 16)

The heart is the most important organ of both the physical and spiritual body. Our Prophet Muḥammad ﷺ said, *"There is a piece of flesh in the body if it becomes good (reformed) the whole body becomes good but if it gets spoilt the whole body gets spoilt and that is the heart."*[64] In the physical realm, if the heart is sound, then the rest of the body will also, by and large, be sound, but if the heart is unhealthy, the rest of the body will suffer. The same applies to the

64 *Ṣaḥīḥ* al-Bukhārī 52

spiritual realm. When the spiritual heart is healthy, our religiosity and spirituality will also be sound, but when the spiritual heart is diseased, problems will begin to occur. Our spiritual heart is far more important than our physical heart because our Prophet Muḥammad ﷺ said, *"Allah does not look to your faces and your wealth, but He looks to your heart and to your deeds."*[65] Most of us spend hours worrying about how we look externally, yet very few of us think about our inner state. Allah does not care about our outer bodies; He cares about the state of our heart.

The Quran describes the heart of the believer as soft, *"... when Allah is mentioned, their hearts become fearful..."*[66] The true believers are those who cry when they listen to the Quran, *"And when they hear what has been revealed to the Messenger, you see their eyes overflowing with tears because of what they have recognised of the Truth..."*[67] They are those whose *īmān* rises when they hear the Quran, *"As for those who believed, it has increased them in faith, while they are rejoicing. But as for those in whose hearts is disease, it has [only] increased them in evil..."*[68] The heart of the believer is gentle, soft and tender and this is the opposite of the hard heart.

The heart has many spiritual diseases, but there is one that is truly the root of all others and for this reason, our scholars have called it the 'mother of all diseases'. It is the cornerstone from which all other diseases come about: the hardness of the heart. Allah mentions the hardness of the heart in several places in the Quran. In *Sūrah al-Baqarah*, we learn that Allah revealed to the Children of Israel one of the greatest miracles by resurrecting a dead man in front of their eyes. In the very next verse, Allah says, *"Then your hearts became hardened after that, being like stones or even harder. For indeed, there are stones from which rivers burst forth, and*

65 *Ṣaḥīḥ* Muslim 2564
66 *al-'Anfāl* 8: 2
67 *al-Mā'idah* 5: 83
68 *at-Tawbah* 9: 124-125

there are some of them that split open and water comes out, and there are some of them that fall down for fear of Allah. Allah is not unaware of what you do."[69] Allah says that their hearts became hard *after* they saw the greatest miracle. After they saw the Red Sea split; after they were saved from Pharaoh; after they saw twelve springs pour forth in the desert and a dead man was resurrected. After having *all* of this, still, their hearts became hard. Realise then that the hardness of the heart is not something coming from ignorance. It is not because they did not believe in Allah or see His Mercy. The hardness of the heart appeared in a religious environment, in the presence of a Prophet, and after seeing the miracles of Allah.

What are the symptoms of a hard heart? The greatest symptom of a hard heart is to simply not care about the relationship an individual has with Allah. We do not enjoy the acts of worship and when we pray or read Quran or we are in a religious gathering, we are zoned out. The prayer becomes routine and monotonous and there is no enjoyment or pleasure. The greatest pleasure that any person can have is the pleasure of having a relationship with Allah. When our Prophet ﷺ was in a situation of distress or troubled by this world, he would say, *"O Bilal, call iqāmah for prayer: give us comfort by it."*[70] Standing in prayer would bring the Prophet ﷺ ease. If we do not feel happiness during the actions of the *ṣalāh*, or we are doing it solely out of routine or habit, then this is a symptom that our heart is hard. Another symptom is that a person does not benefit from advice or being in an Islamic environment. Many times, people with a hard heart become arrogant towards religious gatherings and they look down on the people who participate, thinking themselves superior. An individual whose heart is soft will love to listen to advice from the Quran and *Sunnah*. The final symptom is that a person whose heart is hard

69 *al-Baqarah* 2: 74
70 *Sunan* Abū Dāwūd 4985

habitually commits sins without any sense of conscience or guilt. For the repentant sinner, there is always hope. If they feel guilty after sinning, there is light at the end of the tunnel, but for the one who does not even care that they are sinning, then this is of the worst symptoms of the hardness of the heart.

What are some of the factors that cause the hardness of the heart? The first cause that is explicitly mentioned in the Quran is to ignore the remembrance of Allah. *"And whoever turns away from My remembrance – indeed, he will have a depressed life..."*[71] The remembrance of Allah is the primary nourishment of the spiritual heart and when we remove it, the heart will wither and dry. Another factor that is mentioned is to not follow the laws of Islam or care about them. Allah says, *"For their breaking of the covenant We cursed them and made their hearts hard..."*[72] There is a direct causal linkage: disobedience leads to a hard heart. If we are not praying or obeying the laws of Islam, what do we expect other than to have a hard heart? Allah says, *"Hearts rusted because of what they were doing."*[73] It is the actions that cause the hardening of the hearts. When we commit sins to the point that we do not even care about them anymore, our heart has become hard.

Another cause that makes the heart hard is to follow every single bodily desire. There is a tension between the body and the spirit. When we overfeed the body, the spirit is not given the attention that it deserves. That is why in *Ramaḍān* we purposely minimise the body so that the soul can be increased. The final cause of the hardening of the heart is excess engagement in entertainment and wasting of time. Our Prophet ﷺ said, *"Do not laugh too much..."* Now we know that the Prophet ﷺ would laugh many times during the day, so why is he warning us against laughing?

71 *Ṭā' Hā'* 20: 124
72 *al-Mā'idah* 5: 13
73 *al-Muṭaffifīn* 83: 14

Because, he explained, *"...laughing deadens the heart."*[74] Too much laughing and entertainment, causes the heart to harden.

What steps can we take to ensure that our hearts do not become hard? And if this has already happened, what can we do to make it soft again? The following points are not an exhaustive list but a good place to start to rectify or ensure we are saved from our hearts hardening.

Self-monitor. If someone has a weak heart in the physical world, they will get it monitored and checked. If we find ourselves having the symptoms of the disease of a hard heart, then we need to monitor ourselves. This is done in many ways; of them is to assess the religious aspects of our life. How much is Allah a part of our daily life? How much do we remember Him? How much do we practice Islam? No doubt, the more religious we are, the more it will be shown in our actions. One of the pulses of the state of the heart is to reflect on our personal religiosity.

Additional *nawāfil* worship. First, we need to ensure we establish the *farḍ* (obligatory). Allah told us, *"My slave does not draw closer to Me by anything more beloved to Me than that which I have made obligatory upon him."* Then He said, *"My slave continues to draw closer to Me by doing nawāfil (supererogatory) deeds until I love him."*[75] Increasing the *nawāfil* draws the servant closer to Allah.

Make *dhikr* of Allah. We have seen that neglecting *dhikr* hardens the heart therefore the converse also applies: doing *dhikr* is of the best ways to soften the heart. Allah mentions this in the Quran, when He says, *"...Verily, in*

74 *Sunan* at-Tirmidhī 2305
75 *Ṣaḥīḥ* al-Bukhārī 6502

the remembrance of Allah do hearts find tranquillity."[76] The tranquillity of the heart and the softness of the heart are created by the *dhikr* of Allah. This is the primary food that the soul is nourished upon. We should ask ourselves how much *dhikr* am I making? Am I reciting the *adkhār* of the morning and evening? One of the most important ways to make our heart soft is to immerse it in the *dhikr* of Allah.

Spend time in religious gatherings. Birds of a feather flock together. There are some people who continuously backbite or curse and others who only talk about music or sports. If we are always around these people, what will happen? We will become immersed in that culture. When we spend time around people who remind us of Allah, who talk about the Quran, or are involved with the *ummah,* then no doubt, this will have a positive impact on us. As the Prophet ﷺ said, "*A man is upon the religion of his best friend, so let one of you look at whom he befriends.*"[77] If we find ourselves uncomfortable in our social gatherings, then for the sake of this world and the next, we need to find a better set of friends. We need to spend time with a group of people who bring us closer to Allah. This will make our heart softer.

Make *du'ā'* to Allah. We should constantly make *du'ā'* for anything and everything, but especially for our heart. Allah says in the Quran, "*When our punishment came to them, why did they not call out to Us in du'ā'? Instead their hearts became hard.*"[78] Notice Allah says, '*Why didn't they call out to Us?*' Therefore making *du'ā'* is one of the ways of softening the heart. It is the way we communicate with Allah and when we open that window, our heart feels an

---

76 *ar-Ra'd* 13: 28
77 *Sunan* at-Tirmidhī 2378
78 *al-'An'ām* 6: 43

attachment to Him. The Prophet ﷺ used to say, *"O Turner of the Hearts, keep my heart firm on your religion."*[79]

Contemplate death. We should constantly think of the next world and death. The reality is that none of us likes to think about this. We hear about other people's death, and we do not reflect on the fact that the time will come when it will be our death being informed about. Thinking about death softens the heart and helps us to better prepare for Judgment Day.

Recite the Quran. Reciting the Quran is of the greatest heart softeners. We should make time every day to recite the Book of Allah. The Quran is our spiritual food; it is the greatest *dhikr* and nourishment for the soul. Of the best ways to soften the heart is to make time every day for the recitation of the Quran, even if it is only a few minutes. Let there be a moment in every 24 hours when our hearts feel that relationship with the Book of Allah.

Feeding the poor. A Bedouin came to the Messenger of Allah ﷺ complaining about the hardness of his heart. The Prophet said, *"If you want to soften your heart, then feed the poor and pat the head of the orphan."*[80] One of the easiest ways to soften the heart is to be involved with helping the poor. When there are calamities, we will not want to waste our time doing unbeneficial things. Let us see what is going on in the world, let us be aware, and let us be conscious. We need to ensure that we are physically involved in helping those that have less than us, which will also help to soften our hearts.

79 *Sunan* at-Tirmidhī 3522
80 *Musnad* Aḥmad 7522

There are many things that we can do to soften our hearts and prevent them from becoming hard. Of the most important factors is to understand that we have this disease and to work on ways of curing it. Allah says, *"Has the time not come for those who have believed that their hearts should become humbly submissive at the remembrance of Allah and what has come down of the Truth? And let them not be like those who were given the Scripture before, and a long period passed over them, so their hearts hardened; and many of them were defiantly disobedient."*[81] Now is the time to make our hearts soft with the constant remembrance of Allah.

81 *al-Ḥadīd* 57: 16

Crisis of Knowledge

8

Crisis of Knowledge

رَبِّ زِدنِي عِلمًا

"...My Lord! Increase me in knowledge."

(*Ṭā' Hā'* 20: 114)

There is a hadith recorded by Imam Bukhārī[82], in which the Prophet ﷺ told us about a beautiful incident that happened many thousands of years ago. It involved a Christian monk by the name of Jurayj (George) who isolated himself from society in order to worship Allah. The monks of old would devote their entire lives to worship, wearing the worst of garments and denying themselves any pleasure of this world. They would engage only in prayer, fasting and reciting their holy books. Jurayj was living like this in a monastery, but his mother needed his help. She came to the monastery; as women were not allowed to enter, she called from outside; 'Oh Jurayj! I need your help. Come to me.' Jurayj was praying when he heard his mother and he thought to himself,

82 *Ṣaḥīḥ* al-Bukhārī 3436

'Should I prefer my prayer, or should I respond to the call of my mother?' He decided to continue his prayer and by the time he had finished his mother had left. The second day his mother came again whilst he was standing in prayer, and again, he chose the prayer, thinking that this was piety and righteousness. On the third day his mother called out again and Jurayj continued in his prayer. His mother then became enraged and, in her anger, she made a *duʿāʾ* against him, 'Oh Allah! Do not let Jurayj die until he sees the face of prostitutes.'

We know that Allah listens to the *duʿāʾ* of the parent. A prostitute offered herself to Jurayj, but he repeatedly refused her temptations. Finally, when she could not get any response from him, she became pregnant by a shepherd, and then claimed to the townspeople, 'This is the child of Jurayj.' Jurayj was supposed to be a chaste and holy man who never touched women, and now a prostitute was claiming she had borne his son. The townspeople got angry. They went to his monastery, broke it down and started beating Jurayj with sticks saying, 'How could you do this?' He said, 'What did I do?' They said, 'This prostitute has accused you of fathering her child.' Jurayj immediately remembered the *duʿāʾ* of his mother and said, 'This is the *duʿāʾ* of my mother happening in front of my eyes, that I have been accused of doing this immoral deed.' The townspeople called for Jurayj to be executed. When the time came, he asked to be allowed to pray two last *rakaʿāt*. He prayed, and then he poked the child and said, 'Speak. Who is your father?' The child said, 'My father is the shepherd.' When the people saw this they recognised that a miracle had occurred. They apologised to Jurayj and said they would rebuild his monastery in gold and silver, but he said, 'No, build it with mud and sand as it was and let me continue in my worship.'

There are many benefits and lessons which can be taken from this story, however, the point that I want to emphasise is that in one narration of the hadith, the Prophet ﷺ said, *"If Jurayj had sound knowledge, he would have known that answering his mother was more important than continuing his prayer."*[83] This is one hadith, and there are many others, that prove beyond a shadow of a doubt, that the knowledgeable scholar far exceeds the status of a continual worshipper. Jurayj had devoted himself to worship, but he did not possess true religious knowledge, and this ultimately, led to actions that led to his determent. For us to be able to act correctly, we must have knowledge. It is for this reason that Imam Bukhārī placed the chapter of knowledge before that of actions and speech in his *Ṣaḥīḥ*.

Another profound illustration of the blessings of knowledge is found in the Quran. When Allah told the angels that He would make a creation for the earth that would have free will, they said, *"...Will You place upon it one who causes corruption therein and sheds blood, while we declare Your praise and sanctify You?"*[84] Allah wanted to show that mankind, when pious and righteous, was in fact better in comparison to the angels. How did He prove this? He taught ʾĀdam knowledge that the angels did not have. When the angels saw this they said, *"Exalted are You; we have no knowledge except what You have taught us. Indeed, it is You who is the Knowing, the Wise."*[85] Through knowledge, the superiority of ʾĀdam was manifested.

There are many *āyāt* and hadith that tell us about the blessings of knowledge. Of them is, *"It is only those who have knowledge among His slaves that fear Allah."*[86] No one can reach the level of pure love and fear of Allah, other than those who possess knowledge. Because of this, knowledge is the only thing that Allah commanded the Prophet ﷺ to ask for in large quantity, *"...My*

83 Adab al Mufrad by al-Bukhari
84 *al-Baqarah* 2: 30
85 *al-Baqarah* 2: 32
86 *Fāṭir* 35: 28

Lord, increase me in knowledge."[87] This is the Messenger of Allah being commanded to ask for more knowledge! What does that say about its importance? Allah says in another verse, *"...remember the favour of Allah upon you and what has been revealed to you of the Book and wisdom by which He instructs you..."*[88] This is further illustrated in the hadith, *"When Allah wishes good for someone, He bestows upon him the understanding of religion."*[89] If Allah desires good for you, He gives you the knowledge of Islam. Therefore, the converse also applies, the one who has no interest in Islam or the Islamic sciences has had their share of blessings greatly diminished. The Prophet ﷺ taught us that one of the few things from which we can earn reward from after our death is from the knowledge that people continue to benefit from. We need to ask ourselves, how can we gain this knowledge?

We need to realise, that this is not just about us as individuals; the implications are far wider than that. We are currently facing a crisis of Islamic knowledge in the West. I am very optimistic that the next generation will be much better than their elders in working for community development and fostering harmony with the wider society. What I am concerned about is that Islamically speaking, we are nowhere near the level of scholarship required that will allow us to thrive. For any community to move forward, they need to have *ʿUlemāʾ* (scholars) that are from within that community. This is why Allah says in the Quran, *"And We did not send any messenger except [speaking] in the language of his people..."*[90] Leaders need to be from within their communities otherwise they will not be able to understand their people. We have plenty of complaints about the current generation of religious leaders, but we need to ask ourselves, are we ready to take the torch? Are we ready

87 *Ṭā Hā* 20: 114
88 *al-Baqarah* 2: 231
89 *Ṣaḥīḥ* al-Bukhārī 71
90 *Ibrāhīm* 14: 4

to be a spiritual leader; a *faqīh*, a *muftī*, a *khaṭīb*, or an *imām*? Are we even qualified to lead the prayer? Can we recite the Quran with the proper *tajwīd*? Can we give a basic *khuṭbah*? As long as we have to continue to import our *'Ulemā'* from overseas, the progress of our Islam will be impeded.

It is imperative that we educate ourselves about our religion. We need to understand that 'knowledge' is not something that we either have or we do not have: there are millions of shades of grey in-between. All we need to do is work on improving our shade. Some people travel to study, but we can get to the level of a Student of Knowledge without ever travelling abroad. We need to get out of the mindset/mentality of — *dīn* or *dunyā* — we can do both. We can study medicine or engineering and still make a point of learning about our religion. Even if we can not fully commit and one day become a scholar, we need to make sure that we do not remain ignorant. We must strive to seek Islamic knowledge in whatever way we can.

Where do we start? We need to first look at how we spend our time. We must first identify what time we have available and slot in something beneficial. Do we spend twenty minutes in the morning browsing news articles or social media online? Can we cut it to 5 minutes and use those 15 minutes to learn about our religion? Do we have some travelling time? Can we schedule in during travelling some time for acquiring beneficial knowledge? There is so much that we can do right now to better ourselves in the Islamic Sciences. Here are just a few ideas to get us started:

Find a mentor: A mentor is necessary to guide us because otherwise, we will not know what to study or how to study. We need to find someone who is more knowledgeable than us to recommend where to start.

Listen to a series of talks: There are many series available freely online on platforms like youtube about topics such as the prophets, the *Ṣaḥābah* or *Fiqh*. A series is important because we build on our existing knowledge. We should make time to listen every day until we finish an entire collection. Then listen again to solidify what we know. An important aspect is ensuring we are consistent with our actions.

Read books: Schedule in time, even if it is just 15 minutes a day, to read a book about Islam. In this way, we can continuously build upon our knowledge of our religion.

Study the Quran and *Sunnah*: Without exception, we should read the Quran and hadith on a daily basis. We need to ensure that we read the Quran in Arabic and then its translation in English; it is food for the soul. We also need to ensure that we read books of hadith, even if it is just one hadith a day. A starting place could be with *Forty Hadith* and *Riyāḍ al-Ṣāliḥīn* by Imam Nawawī.

Study the *Sīrah*: We know so much about the lives of celebrities and famous athletes and so little about our the life of our beloved Prophet ﷺ. We must study the *Sīrah* of our beloved Prophet, peace and blessings of Allah be upon him. We, therefore, must-read books, listen to lectures and prioritise deepening our knowledge about the best man who ever lived.

Enrol in an Institute: There are so many institutes that are teaching Islamic Studies. There is no shortage of choice, therefore we should find one and enrol. We spend so much time studying worldly knowledge; we should equally make time to study our religion.

If we all were to do these things, slowly but surely we will rise-up in the shades of grey to reach a position where we are able to make a contribution to the development of Islam within our local community and help alleviate this crisis of knowledge that we are currently facing.

The State We're In

9

The State We're In

وَمَن يَتَوَكَّل عَلَى اللَّهِ فَهُوَ حَسْبُهُ ۚ إِنَّ اللَّهَ بَالِغُ أَمْرِهِ ۚ
قَدْ جَعَلَ اللَّهُ لِكُلِّ شَيْءٍ قَدْرًا

"...And whoever relies upon Allah
then He is sufficient for him.
Indeed, Allah will accomplish His purpose.
Allah has already set for everything
a [decreed] extent."

(*aṭ-Ṭalāq* 65: 3)

Many of us are struggling to make sense of what is currently happening in the world today. Muslims always seem to be in the news in a negative way, and it is not just the terrorism and violence - it is that Muslim countries seem to be repressive and lagging behind the Western world. Civilisations that have rejected Islam appear, on the outside, to be flourishing. This dichotomy and disparity between the Muslim world and the Western world can cause people to ask, 'If our religion is true, then why are our civilisations so backwards?' These types of questions can affect people's īmān and even lead them to question their faith. For this reason, it is important to gain a deeper understanding of the situation we find ourselves in as Muslims today and to do that we need to look more closely at three areas: history, politics and theology.

In order to understand today, we need to understand what happened yesterday because we can not isolate today's events from what happened in the past. If we look back even one hundred years, the world was a very different place. In 1915 we still had a Caliphate. It was not by any means the greatest, but it represented a continuous legacy of Islamic civilisation that went back 1350 years. When the British and Allied forces launched their first major attack against the Ottoman Empire, they aimed straight for Istanbul, the seat of the Caliphate. This attack would eventually lead to the collapse of the political structure that began with the Prophet ﷺ and remained unbroken all the way up to Abdul Hamid II.

The British used the tactic of divide and conquer to succeed in their approach. They introduced the concept of nationalism, which had been unknown in the *ummah* before this point in time. They promised the Arabs that if they fought the Turks they would be given an independent Arab state stretching from Iraq to North Africa and incorporating Jerusalem and Palestine. Under the false promise that they would eventually be given charge, one group of Muslims openly revolted, joined the British and fought against the Ottomans. But even as the British promised the Arabs freedom and independence, they had already agreed with France and Russia on how to carve up the Muslim world between themselves. The borders of the modern nation-states of Jordan, Syria, Lebanon, Iraq and Arabia — practically the entire map of the Middle East — were literally drawn up between a Frenchman and an Englishman, in what is known as the Sykes-Picot Agreement. Along with the public declaration to the Arabs, and the private promise to the French and the Russians, the British made a third secret pact, known as the Balfour Declaration, with the World Zionist Federation. They promised them the creation of an independent Jewish homeland in the heart of Palestine if they supported the British financially in WWI. These are the three promises that every Muslim should be aware of: the public promise to the Arabs, the private negotiation with the French and the Russians and the secret negotiation with the World Zionist Federation.

As WWI drew to an end just over one hundred years ago, Allied forces entered Damascus, then Jerusalem, then Baghdad and eventually Istanbul itself. Each one of these cities represented a bastion of Islamic rule, and Jerusalem represented the holiest land to all three faiths - Islam, Christianity and Judaism. Symbolically, the entire Caliphate and its history were captured in the span of a few years. The modern map of the Middle East as we know it today did not organically come out of the will of the people of that region. The very notion of nation-states and nationalism, the carving of borders in countries that are now the source of so much conflict, are all the legacies of foreign intervention. The entire Palestinian-Israeli conflict is nothing other than one foreign entity (Great Britain) deciding to give someone else's land (Arab and Muslim) over to a third party (European Jewry). As we look at the conflicts in that region, we cannot ignore the series of dominoes that occurred previously. We must study history, in particular colonialism and WWI and its impact on the Middle East, in order to understand why these conflicts exist within the Muslim lands today.

The second area we need to understand is politics. The world is full of a few very big political players, who set the rules, and many smaller players, who try to navigate their way through those rules. Politics is not a level playing field. It is a dirty game and it is the masses, not the rich and elite, who suffer as a result. Sadly, in many cases, it is Muslim lands that have borne the brunt of this suffering, especially those that are now experiencing violence and Islamic radicalism. This is not to justify or exonerate radicalism. We all recognise that radical groups are not representative of our faith. We are not blaming others for their crimes, rather we are just trying to understand, where does this violence come from? It does not come from the Quran; it is not from our tradition. There are other factors that we need to take into account. Take the example of the Arab Spring. The New York Times detailed how America was involved behind the scenes, using its influence to dictate how one group of people was removed from office and others engineered in. It is not a coincidence that the situation in the Middle East is as volatile as it is, because it is not representing the will of the people. It is not a coincidence that radicalism typically emerges from places that have repressive regimes. It is not a coincidence that ISIS come from Iraq and Syria. Before we blame Muslims, and only Muslims, take a step back and study history and politics. They will tell us a lot more about our current situation than the religion of Islam. This leads to my final point: theology.

How do we understand, from a theological perspective, why people who believe in Allah seem to be suffering so much? Why are our lands so backward and repressed? Maybe there are historical and political reasons, but still, if we are believers in Allah and His Messenger, how do we understand a loving and merciful God testing His people in this manner? This is of course a very deep philosophical question, one that deals with the existence of evil and how we understand it.

As Muslims, we believe that the good that comes out of evil and suffering outweighs the bad. Any suffering endured by a righteous person in this world, any problem, pain, or grief, will earn a great reward in the next life. Our Prophet ﷺ said, *"On the*

Day of Resurrection, when people who had suffered affliction are given their reward, those who were healthy will wish that their skins had been cut to pieces with scissors when they were in the world."[91] This understanding enables us to endure suffering, by demonstrating patience. We believe that evil is returned with good, and we also believe that good comes out of evil. This is because one of the purposes of the existence of suffering is that it causes the good in us to come out in order to combat it. How can we be generous to the poor if there is no poverty? How can we help orphans if there are no orphans to help? How can we feed the hungry unless there are people that need food? Suffering enables us to gain the reward of Allah through patience when we are afflicted, and through helping those who are suffering when we are not.

Know that the ultimate sign of Truth is not how many PhDs or Nobel Prize winners exist within the Muslim lands or how large a nation's GDP is. Those mechanisms have a role to play, but they are not the ultimate criterion of success. The best of people, the Prophets and the *Ṣaḥābah* after them, did not have these honours. What did they have? Spirituality, ethics and a purpose of life. This is what we have to give. We know the purpose of our existence. We are the ones who have the most morality, who are the most generous, who respect our elders and who live with dignity and decency. Those values that are far more precious than the material blessings of this world. As Muslims, we have been made a witness unto mankind. We are tasked with conveying the Truth, preaching morality, embodying justice, epitomising nobility and most importantly, representing the Prophetic message. Be proud of our spiritual heritage. Realise that the gift we have been given, the gift of faith, is something so precious that it deserves to be shared with the rest of the world. Islam is the most prized possession and it is the ultimate measure of success.

---

91 al-Tirmidhī, 2402

Our Times, Our Challenges

10

Our Times, Our Challenges

وَإِن تُطِعۡ أَكۡثَرَ مَن فِي ٱلۡأَرۡضِ يُضِلُّوكَ عَن سَبِيلِ ٱللَّهِ

"And if you obey most of those upon the earth, they will mislead you from the way of Allah…"

(*al-'An'ām* 6: 116)

How do we navigate our way through the maze of modern controversies? Fanaticism, liberalism and calls for the 'reform' of Islam are but a few of the issues that we face in our times. When facing challenges such as these, we need to reflect on incidents from early Islam to find the guidelines that we should follow in order to ensure that we remain 'rightly guided'.

In a hadith narrated in Abū Dāwūd, a group of *Ṣaḥābah* went out on a military expedition and in the course of fighting one of them got a severe head wound. On the journey back, he woke from his sleep in a state of *janābah* (ritual impurity) and needed to pray the *fajr* prayer. The weather was extremely cold, he had an open wound and the question arose, did he need to make *ghusl* (full body ablution)? There was no person of knowledge amongst them. One of the *Ṣaḥābah* said that the Quran clearly stated that you have to do *ghusl* for this type of impurity, and he did not know of any exception for a wound. So the man took a full bath, the wound festered, and he eventually died. When the Prophet ﷺ heard of this, he said, *"They have killed him, may Allah curse them!"*[92] We read in another hadith that when the Prophet ﷺ cursed a believer out of anger, Allah would change it into a blessing for them, so he did not literally curse them, but he was angry that they had given a *fatwā* that was wrong, and that the result had been a *Ṣaḥābah* 's death. The Prophet ﷺ then said, *"Is not the cure for ignorance to ask questions?"*[93] This hadith shows us the dangers of overzealousness, which are all too common amongst some segments of our community today. Some brothers and sisters make Islam so difficult that they eventually burnt out. They do not realise that for every rule, there were exceptions; for every verse, there were clauses to get out. The *Ṣaḥābī* did not have that knowledge, and in his zealousness to be Quranic, he unintentionally went against Islamic principles. We all know people like that.

Another incident shows us the opposite approach. In the time of ʿUmar ibn al-Khaṭṭāb, may Allah be pleased with him, there was a man who was well known for his services to the community. He had fought battles with the Prophet ﷺ but he was not a person of knowledge. He read the verse, *"There is not upon those who believe and do righteousness blame concerning what they have eaten if they fear Allah and believe and do righteous deeds..."*[94] and decided that the Quran allowed the drinking alcohol if he was otherwise righteous. He took one verse, which was open to interpretation, and he used it to trump every other verse, every hadith and the

92 *Sunan* Abū Dāwūd 337
93 *Sunan* Abū Dāwūd 337
94 *al-Māʾidah* 5: 93

unanimous consensus of the *Ṣaḥābah*, that all prohibited the drinking of alcohol. He was brought in front of *'Umar*, drunk, and he tried to use this verse as an excuse. ʿUmar punished him for the sin of drinking because this interpretation was nowhere within the acceptable spectrum of opinions in Islam. The methodology the man used, the *uṣūl*, was nonsensical and it was not accepted as an excuse.

What this shows us is that from the beginning, we have had ultra-fanaticism and ultra-liberalism, but they have always been at the peripheries of Islam. The bulk of the *ummah* and Islamic scholarship has always been within these two extremes. One of the primary ways to deal with the problems of our times is to ignore the extremist voices on both sides and to concentrate on the consensus of what the Prophet ﷺ called the bulk of the *ummah*, or the *Jamāʿah*. Our Prophet ﷺ said, *"Allah will not cause my ummah to agree on falsehood. Allah's Hand is over the Jamāʿah, and whoever deviates, he deviates to the Fire."*[95] When we look at Islamic scholarship we can clearly see, that from the beginning of time there has been a spectrum of permissibility, a spectrum of opinions that scholars have held, and then there are the fringes that by and large have been rejected.

When we are navigating through a modern controversy we should always look at who is giving the *fatwā*. Look at that individual's track record, look at their credibility, look at their peers and look at their acceptance within the *ummah*. All of these things are signs in the eyes of Allah, and they are methods that we can use to gauge the veracity and the authenticity of an opinion. We are living at times of pseudo-scholarship, when people who have never studied the *Sharīʿah*, but have the gift of the gab and know how to mesmerise audiences, are assumed to be scholars. Would we go to a

95 *Sunan* at-Tirmidhī 2167

doctor who had only studied from Wikipedia? No. Then why is our religion cheaper than our life? We need to educate ourselves about authentic Islamic scholarship and how to seek our guidance from it.

The youth growing up in the West today should also realise that just as they question Islam, and the scholars, they should also be brave enough to question their own paradigm and the dominant narrative from within which their questions are emanating. We need to be cognizant of the effects of being born at a particular time, in a particular society and a particular culture. This fact automatically causes us to absorb values through osmosis and interaction, and some of those values might not be Islamic. Be brave enough to question the mainstream understandings. Question the questions just as much, or even more, than we are willing to question the Islamic tradition.

Morality and ethics in the mainstream Western environment evolve over time, but in Islam morality and ethics are always stable. One of the things that we are taught in the Western environment is to be tolerant, to be liberal and to accept differences of opinion. This is the dominant narrative and we think this is appropriate. Yet we see clear double standards over and over again. Only being tolerant to those whom we approve of is not real tolerance. We must remember that the majority does not decide morality; Allah does. He tells us in the Quran, *"And if you obey most of those upon the earth, they will mislead you from the way of Allah..."*[96]

I have been asked by young men and women about controversies that cause them to doubt their faith. They are mostly about trivial issues in the grand scheme of things. Of them is the age of Aisha, may Allah be pleased with her, at the time of her marriage to the Prophet. They are confused and feel they do not know how to defend the Prophet ﷺ because they do not think

96 *al-ʾAnʿām* 6: 116

what he did was 'ethically' right. The reason why they are so certain that it is unethical and immoral is that they believe that times have changed. They are back projecting our standards of ethical and moral law onto 7th century Arabia. For the bulk of human history, marriages took place at a young age. In every state in America only a hundred years ago, the age of marriage was in the early teens. People were married at an earlier age in the past because they matured earlier physically and mentally, and because lifespans were shorter. When Shakespeare wrote Romeo and Juliet, their ages were 14 and 13; it was the equivalent of our 19 and 18 today. Nobody is saying that a young girl of our times should be married, times have clearly changed. However, to assume that our Prophet ﷺ was immoral is a grave error. We need to question the question. We need to contextualise, rather than projecting modern problems onto a culture of fourteen centuries ago.

Similarly, with the issue of the Theory of Evolution, we need to understand the Western paradigm, as well as our own. There is no problem with most parts of the Theory of Evolution other than as it relates to humans. The earth is older than 6000 years, there were dinosaurs and people painted cave painting 30,000 years ago; these are all facts. How then do we reconcile this with the Quranic creation story? The Quran is not metaphorical, and we can affirm that all life came from one source; nothing is random. The Quran tells us that ʾĀdam was created, and we can fit this into the bigger picture of evolutionary theory. When it was our turn, Allah inserted man, fully created, to fit perfectly into the wider system. The children of ʾĀdam are a unique creation and many things in science prove this point. Of them are language, knowledge and the arts. All of this fits within the wider Quranic narrative.

What we need to understand is that there is a tension between the East and the West and how they view the relationship between faith and science. The Catholic Church prevented education and clashed with science. The Renaissance then changed the way Europe thought of education until Western culture, by and large, agreed with the fact that the Bible was not a book of science. The West, therefore, believes that when science flourishes, society will flourish, and when religion is in charge, society will suffer. This is projected onto Islamic culture, but our experience is different. The flourishing of Islam and the sciences occurred together under the *Khilāfah*. When we were faithful to our tradition and our Book, Allah blessed us. As our political states declined so too did our sciences, but Muslims never lost faith in their Book: Christians did. They rejected the literalism of their scripture because for them it caused problems. As Muslims, we believe that the Quran is the Divine uncorrupted Word of Allah. When a Western mind hears this, they think that this is the belief that held them back and that Islam needs to reform. There is a fundamental paradigm clash between the West and Islam in this regard. We need to understand that paradigm and the questions that emanate from it and realise that they do not apply to us. The same goes for so many other issues.

As we navigate our way through the challenges of our times, there are three things that we need to do. Firstly, study our tradition. Educate ourselves with Islamic knowledge. Find the *ʿUlemāʾ* in our local community and study with them. We need to learn from their wisdom and experience. We need to ensure that we stick to the majority opinion and keep away from the extremes. Secondly, we need to question the dominant narrative. Question the thinking of the place and times that we happen to be born into. Question the values of liberalism and where it is going to lead: eventually everything will become permissible. Even Nietzsche himself predicted that if we eliminated God, there would be no morality left and life would eventually become meaningless. If we remove belief in Allah and His guidance, what is left? Finally, we need to make *duʿāʾ* for Allah to guide us on the Straight Path and ask Him for *hidāyah* (guidance). ʿUmar, may Allah be pleased with him, used to make the *duʿāʾ*, *"O Allah, show me the truth as truth, and allow me to follow it, and show me evil as evil and take me away from it."*[97] Imagine if ʿUmar had to make this *duʿāʾ*, then how much more are we in need of it today?

97 *Sharḥ al-Muntahá al-Irādāt* Buhūtī 3/497

Lost Faith

11
Lost Faith

قَالَ رَسُولُ اللَّهِ صَلَّى اللَّهُ عَلَيْهِ وَسَلَّمَ دَعْ مَا يَرِيبُكَ إِلَى
مَا لَا يَرِيبُكَ فَإِنَّ الصِّدْقَ طُمَأْنِينَةٌ وَإِنَّ الْكَذِبَ رِيبَةٌ

"Leave that which makes you doubt
for that which does not make you doubt,
for Truth leads to reassurance
and lies lead to uncertainty."

(at-Tirmidhī 2442)

Young people today are going through problems and challenges unlike those of previous generations. Islam may be the fastest-growing religion in the world, but there is a dark side that is often ignored or neglected by the wider community: atheism and agnosticism are on the rise. Every one of us knows of someone who has gone through a crisis of faith and perhaps even someone who has left Islam because of it.

Recently, I spoke to someone who had renounced Islam. He had been a prominent member of his community, a youth counsellor and regular at the *masjid.* All of a sudden he dropped out for a year and then announced that he was no longer a Muslim. He asked me the standard questions about issues he was finding ethically problematic about the Quran, the *Sunnah* and the *Sīrah.* He is not the only one to ask me these questions or to consider leaving Islam because of them. We need to reflect on the thinking behind this phenomenon more deeply in order to understand how to properly address it.

We need to realise that Allah created us with three primary needs: physical, spiritual and intellectual. Our physical needs are that we need to eat, drink, and breathe and if we do not have these things we will die. We also have spiritual needs that must be fulfilled and if they are not, we will experience a sense of meaninglessness, emptiness and even depression because we have no sense of a higher purpose in life. When we do not have a higher spiritual goal, we create another goal and make it the highest. That is why in our times there are so many causes that people are passionate about be it ethical issues, environmental or animal issues. People want to have a more noble goal, it is ingrained in us to do so, and Islam answers to that spiritual need. Lastly, we have intellectual needs that have to be fulfilled: our curiosity must be met. Islam comes with enough for all three of these needs. It tells us how to live our lives physically and spiritually, and it provides us with the answers for meaningful questions like, 'What is the purpose of life?'

The problem comes when we take one of these three functions and use them to trump the others. In our times, it is the issue of rationality. We use our intellect to try and understand every minutia of Islam, and if we can not understand it, we end up rejecting the entire faith. Does this mean that there are things in Islam that are irrational? No. Islam does not come with anything that is irrational, but it comes with certain things that are supra-rational, in that rationality does not have a role in judging whether they are valid or not. We will never understand why we pray five times a day and not four or six. It might not be something that we can fully understand rationally due to our limited intellect, but neither is it irrational.

The role of the intellect and reason in Islam is a deep and detailed topic. Ibn Taymiyyah, in his work *Averting the Conflict between Reason and Revealed Tradition*, discusses the relationship between reason and revelation and critiques the idea that reason alone can arrive at Truth. He brings forth many examples, first and foremost amongst them being the impossibility of even defining what 'reason' is, what 'rationality' is, and what is 'intellectual'. What is intellectual for us today might not have been intellectual a generation ago and what is rational for us today was not rational one hundred years before. Rationality itself changes from society to society and from time and place, so there is nothing that we can judge rationality by in and of itself. In fact, in our own lives, how many times have we undertaken a course of action thinking, 'This is so logical, this is so rational', and the next day, the next week, the next month, the next year, we look back and we say, 'What a bad decision I made. How could I have thought that?' How then can we then take 'reason' to be something that is above and beyond anything, thinking we can derive the ultimate Truth from it?

Does this mean that Islam has nothing to do with reason? No. Allah tells us to think and to ponder over His Signs. If we look at the Quranic commands to think and reflect, they never tell us to challenge Allah's Revelation. Rather, the Quran addresses non-Muslims and says, 'Think! Is Islam true or not? Is the Prophet true or not? Is this Book from Allah or not?' Once we have used our intellect to come to the conclusion that the Quran is a Book from Allah and that the Prophet Muḥammad ﷺ is a true prophet, we are not supposed to use our reason to question every law and wisdom of Islam. They are beyond the scope of our intellect to understand. If we rely solely on our questions and think that our mind itself will be able to answer them, then we are doomed to fail. We should judge Islam based on theology, on the purpose of life and on the fact that the Quran is a Book from Allah. Once we have established that these things are true, we will then accept the Message as it is.

Islam caters to more than just intellectual questions. Far more profound is the fact that it caters to our inner spirituality, the *fiṭrah* (original nature) that Allah created us upon. The Prophet ﷺ said, *"Every child is born upon the fiṭrah."*[98] The *fiṭrah* is a source of intuitive knowledge and not knowledge that is gained from society. We are born knowing certain facts, for example, right from wrong and morality from immorality. Every child knows that to be good is good and to be bad is bad. Lying, cheating and stealing are not good and a child knows this because it is in the *fiṭrah*. The *fiṭrah* also tells us that there is one God and that He alone is worthy of worship. The inner consciousness of the Muslim is at ease with the belief that Islam is true because the *fiṭrah* knows it to be true.

When questions arise, we need to ask ourselves, 'Does every single question about Islam have to have a rational answer?' We assume the answer is yes, and this is one of the biggest issues of our times. The answers to doubts are not necessarily all rational; some of them come from the *fiṭrah* and science does not take this into account. A simple example of this is the existence of God. In our times, we have intelligent people denying God's existence. This is because belief in God is not purely an intellectual exercise. It is

98 *Ṣaḥīḥ* al-Bukhārī 1292

in fact an understanding of the *fiṭrah*. Allah says, *"And [mention] when your Lord took from the children of ʾĀdam — from their loins — their descendants and made them testify of themselves, [saying to them], "Am I not your Lord?" They said, "Yes, we have testified..."*[99] The understanding of the existence of God is something ingrained in us: we can not scientifically prove it exists, but it is there. That is why the Quran gives paganism, worshipping other gods besides Allah, more intellectual credit than atheism. There are over five hundred verses addressed to pagans in the Quran and only one or two to atheists. As Ibn Taymiyyah (d. 1328) said, *"How do you expect me to go and find proofs for Allah's existence, when everything around me is screaming His existence?"*[100] There is no point in trying to pursue complicated proofs. Nobody ever converted based on philosophical arguments. Atheists refuse to believe, but that is not an intellectual problem, it is a spiritual one. The question then becomes, 'If we cannot understand the wisdom of Allah, are we still going to believe in Him or not?' and that is the belief in the unseen. To 'submit' to Allah — which is literally the meaning of Islam — requires a level of humility of the soul, and a recognising of the limits of oneself and one's intellect.

But all hope is not lost. Recently, an acquaintance of mine who had converted to Islam, and then left, reaccepted the faith. When I asked him why he reaccepted after leaving the faith, he told me that a parent had passed away in front of his eyes. The reality of life and death and the Truth of Islam all came back to him at that moment. He knew there was no alternative but to submit to Allah. If someone we know has left the faith, we can be sure that if there is an ounce of sincerity in them, they will eventually come back. If we ourselves are having doubts, or we know someone who is, know that the most important thing that we can do is to sincerely call

---

99 *al-ʾAʿrāf* 7: 172
100 Madarij al-Salikin 1-60

out to the One who created us, and for us to be guided onto the Straight Path. Never underestimate the power of *duʿāʾ*. Remember that whoever sincerely wants to be guided, will be guided. If we are sincere, Allah will not forsake us.

Fear of Others

12
Fear of Others

وَلَنَبلُوَنَّكُم بِشَيءٍ مِنَ الخَوفِ وَالجوعِ وَنَقصٍ مِنَ
الأَموالِ وَالأَنفُسِ وَالثَّمَراتِ ۗ وَبَشِّرِ الصّابِرينَ

"And certainly,
We shall test you with something of
fear, hunger, loss of wealth, lives and fruits,
but give glad tidings to the patient."

(*al-Baqarah* 2: 155)

At present, we are living in dire times. Muslims across the globe are being persecuted because of their faith, anti-Muslim legislation is being passed, false accusations are being made and intolerance of Islam is rising. There is paranoia everywhere. We know that those who do not learn from history are doomed to repeat it, so I want to share something that happened in America just seventy years ago.

In the 1940s there was mass incarceration of Japanese Americans. The US military rounded up more than a hundred thousand people, just because they were of Japanese heritage. These were not immigrants who had recently arrived; many of them were second and third-generation Americans, including some who had just one grandparent who was Japanese. They were held in open-air prisons for years without charge, or any idea of when their ordeal would end.

How did this happen? To get the full perspective, we need to understand what happened in the 1890s, when tens of thousands of Chinese people came to work in America. They came legally, taking jobs that Americans would not take, and primarily worked building railroads. Even though the Chinese were comparatively small in number, Americans felt afraid of a people of a different race, religion, language and culture. This fear was tapped into by the newspapers and exaggerated, leading to campaigns against the Chinese, including cartoons that displayed them in derogatory terms. The broader public was made to feel that there was an imminent threat from Chinese Americans unless they put a stop to it. They called this 'Yellow Fear'.

Once the hatred had been fomented, politicians rode the wave of xenophobia to boost their popularity. They banked in on hatred and bigotry propagating racist views about the Chinese and people voted them in. In California, a Senator ran for office with the motto 'The Chinese Must Go' and won by a landslide, even though at the time Chinese people represented less than 1% of the population of that state. Laws were enacted that prohibited marriage between Chinese and non-Chinese Americans and zones were allocated in which Chinese people could live. Then in 1917, the government issued the Chinese Exclusion Act, informally known as the 'Yellow Act', which effectively banned immigration to America from any countries other than Caucasian ones.

The fear that had been fomented against one group — the Chinese — was used to spread fear against another — the Japanese — after the bombing of Pearl Harbour during World War II. President Roosevelt issued an Executive Order to imprison all Japanese people in isolated camps, to prevent espionage. Japanese Americans were identified by their neighbours, taken from their homes in the middle of the night, and imprisoned without charge. This mass incarceration was fought through the legal system on multiple levels, until one case reached the Supreme Court where it was ruled that it was permissible, in extreme circumstances, to suspend the law. The Supreme Court of America made it legal to arrest a person, without any charge, and imprison them in a concentration camp simply because one of their grandparents was Japanese. This occurred just one generation ago.

When America first began preaching hatred of Chinese people, other Western countries latched on. New Zealand, Australia, Germany and England all began anti-Chinese campaigns, even though they were not experiencing large-scale Chinese immigration. The Western culture found it convenient to scapegoat a group of people, creating a common enemy that would unite them. This created what is known as a 'confirmation bias'; when we hear what we already believe, it makes us certain that what we believe is true. When we keep on perpetuating the same lies, people begin to believe them.

If all of this feels frightening familiar, it is because we see the same phenomena taking place concerning Muslims today. Western nations have made Islam a major issue. European parliaments are banning the wearing of *niqāb* and *ḥijāb*. America has banned immigration from several Muslim-majority countries and Switzerland has outlawed the construction of minarets. This is confirmation bias in action, creating a sense of an imminent threat that needs to be repelled.

What happens when everyone has been whipped into a frenzy? The legislation begins. In Nazi Germany in the 1920s, the Jews were dehumanised in the same way that Muslims are being dehumanised today. They were declared to be a 'fifth column' that was looking to destroy the fabric of German society and establish their own laws. Similarly, today many people in the West believe that unless they stop Muslims, they will seek to establish *Sharīʿah* Law in Western lands. The media and politicians make people believe that Muslims are coming to get them. Unless we stop that stereotype, and the hatred and fear, we too may witness the final horrifying stage that the Japanese and the Jews experienced. We have already seen the stereotyping, the caricatures and the legislation. What is left? The final stage is rounding people up and doing something physical.

We live sheltered lives with the sense that we are many in number and that everything is OK, but we are in fact a dismal minority in Western lands. Despite this, the broader public has made us a staple issue and politicians are demonising us with such regularity that we should be alarmed. In the twenty years that led to the Holocaust, there was a sustained, systematic campaign to dehumanise Jews and desensitise the broader public to what was going to take place. What we are seeing happening to Muslims now is a necessary precursor to a future Holocaust. Until and unless we understand that our safety and the safety of our children and grandchildren may be at risk, what will make us act? Unless we take action, the next stage might be very terrifying, and we seek Allah's protection from that. May Allah forbid, and may He protect us, but if another disaster or calamity, similar in magnitude or worse than what happened on 9/11 were to happen today, just imagine the consequences.

Why is this happening? Why are politicians and the media creating this storm? It is a well-documented fact that the people who propagate these lies against Muslims know full well that they are lies. They are doing this only for political expediency. Just like in Nazi Germany, when Himmler used this tactic with the Jews, politicians are teaching people that Muslims are a threat to their safety, exaggerating the threat, and then portraying themselves as the saviour. Who comes out the winner? The politicians. This tactic, of creating Muslims as the imagined enemy, is a tactic of distraction. Politicians do not want people to think about the state of the economy, the underfunded education system, or the problem of healthcare. This tactic works extremely well amongst the uneducated masses. We need to understand that the average person who says they hate Muslims, is simply believing the lies that they are told. We cannot respond to hate with hate. We need to educate people about the reality. The real guilty people are the ones that fed them those lies, knowing full well they were not true in the first place. We have to empathise with our neighbour because if we respond to his hatred with hatred, then we have proven his point.

What can we do? There is a religious response to this question involving *īmān*, *taqwā* and *duʿāʾ* that I have dealt with in many other places, so I will not address that here. The times we are in call for us to do something beyond the *masjid*, and it is those actions that I want to elaborate on. Firstly, we need to understand our circle of impact — our friends, our colleagues and our neighbours — and know that no-one can impact those people as we can. We represent Islam to them and if we fail in representing it well, then Islam has failed in their eyes. Actions speak louder than words. We need to make it a point to show our neighbours and our colleagues the beauty of Islam and the honesty and mercy of our religion. Our Prophet ﷺ was known to be truthful before he was known as a Messenger. Whether we like it or not, we represent our beloved Prophet ﷺ in the eyes of the average person. We need to make our conduct the best amongst our friends and colleagues. We need to make it a point to do it for the sake of Allah and Allah will bless us for our actions and make the task easy for us.

Secondly, we need to understand that Islam is more than just rituals and theology. There is a social aspect to our religion that necessitates that we stand up against injustice in our societies. From the earliest days of Islam, the Prophet ﷺ spoke out against issues like female infanticide and economic injustice. These were moral issues, not theological ones. We need to follow his example and take a vested interest in the society around us. Racism, homelessness and access to healthcare are all Islamic issues. Sadly, for many of us, local issues are not considered Islamic and fundraising for a humanitarian crisis abroad is much easier than trying to raise money for a local cause. It is as if we think that local issues have nothing to do with us, but it is a part of our Islamic duty to play an active role in the society we live in and to speak up against injustice.

Thirdly, we must fight the system, from within the system, using the system. We need to support local organisations that are fighting for the rights of Muslims. We all know of cases where Muslims are being prosecuted unfairly. These are legal cases which are seeking to set precedents that will affect us all. For this reason, scholars have agreed that such legal costs are in fact *zakāh* eligible. We should support these cases financially for the sake of Islam. One case can secure the rights of millions of Muslims and clear the path for our children in the future.

These are indeed dire times that we are living in and history shows us this only too well. We need to be alarmed, educate ourself, and let this be a wake-up call to action, both personal and political. We need to strive hard to be the best Muslim that we can be. Our aim should be to emulate the Prophet ﷺ in his truthfulness, compassion and commitment to social justice. Collectively, we need to work for the betterment of society, fight injustice and support the oppressed. Our actions will improve our own lives and the lives of those around us. They will expose the lies people tell about Muslims, and ultimately, earn the reward of Allah.

The Wisdom of Pandemics

13

The Wisdom of Pandemics

عَنِ النَّبِيِّ صلى الله عليه وسلم قَالَ " إِنَّ عِظَمَ الْجَزَاءِ مَعَ عِظَمِ الْبَلاَءِ وَإِنَّ اللَّهَ إِذَا أَحَبَّ قَوْمًا ابْتَلاَهُمْ فَمَنْ رَضِيَ فَلَهُ الرِّضَا وَمَنْ سَخِطَ فَلَهُ السَّخَطُ

"The greatest reward comes from the greatest trial. When Allah loves a people, He tests them. Whoever accepts that wins His pleasure, but whoever is discontent with that earns His wrath."

(at-Tirmidhī 2396)

The entire world has been drastically affected by the pandemic of coronavirus (COVID-19). It has caused unprecedented disruption to our daily lives, preventing travel, closing workplaces and forcing us into social isolation. During great trials such as this, the believer should always look for wisdom and blessings and there are many lessons that we can learn: what follows are seven of them.

The first wisdom of a pandemic is that it teaches us to be humble and realise that only Allah is All-Powerful. The virus has put fear in the hearts of people all over the world, yet it is something so small that it cannot even be seen with the naked eye. In fact, it is the smallest manifestation of any creation and needs to be magnified at least 100,000 times just to be able to see it. As Allah says, "*...He creates that which you do not know.*"[101] Despite all of our technology and development, something this small has brought our societies to a standstill. This is a profound reminder of the fact that we do not have ultimate control over our lives: it is Allah who has control. This realisation should make us humble ourselves in front of the almighty power of Allah.

The second wisdom is that it reminds us of our mortality. Allah tells us in the Quran, "*We did not grant to any man before you eternity...*"[102] All too often we forget that death is real. We have become so comfortable in this *dunyā* and so complacent with our riches that we forget the Hereafter. Calamities are a wake-up call to remind us that none of us will live forever. Inevitably, "*Every soul will taste death...*"[103] When pandemics come and surround us with death, our minds begin to think about the Hereafter. This wakes us from our slumber and reminds us that this life is only temporary. Hard hearts, then become soft, and in this is a blessing from Allah.

The third wisdom that this calamity teaches us is the illusion of the notion that some types of people are better than others. A pandemic affects all of humanity and shows us the foolishness of racism and the superiority complex. The Prophet ﷺ told us that, "*All of the people are the children of ʾĀdam, and ʾĀdam was created from dust.*"[104] We think that our tribe, our race or our nation-state Is better than others, but this virus reminds us that we are

101 *an-Naḥl* 16: 8
102 *al-ʾAnbiyāʾ* 21: 34
103 *Āl ʿImrān* 3: 185
104 *Sunan* at-Tirmidhī 3955

all human and all equally susceptible. The only thing that truly separates us is the state of our hearts.

The fourth wisdom of a pandemic is that it shows us is that this *dunyā* and the wealth and blessings that come with it are not the ultimate signs of success. If someone has all the riches of this world, it does not mean that Allah is pleased with them, and if someone has this *dunyā* taken away, it does not mean that Allah is angry. It is the Hereafter that is a full manifestation of Allah's pleasure. The fact that people who seem to be good and righteous are struck with calamities, and people who seem to be evil or bad are escaping without harm, should make us realise that this *dunyā* is not a place where justice will prevail: ultimate justice is for the Hereafter. Allah says in the Quran, *"And fear a trial which will not strike those who have wronged amongst you exclusively..."*[105] This virus strikes us all. It is our reaction that determines our piety, not the affliction itself. If we are afflicted with the virus, we should not interpret this as Allah being displeased with us. On the contrary, our Prophet ﷺ said of plagues, *"They are a punishment which Allah sends upon whomsoever He wills, but Allah has made it a mercy to the believers."*[106] This pandemic can be a blessing for us if we respond with *ṣalāh, duʿāʾ* and *istighfār* (seeking forgiveness), knowing that Allah forgives sins because of calamities.

The fifth wisdom that we see is that a pandemic makes selfish people realise they need others. Many of us want to live isolated lives, but when we fall sick we need the help of a supportive family and community. It has made us understand that we are all in this together. We see the importance of being part of a wider system that has civil order to keep things running smoothly. We need governments that keep checks and balances to make sure that people do not descend into chaos. When Islam came to Makkah,

105 *al-ʾAnfāl* 8: 25
106 *Ṣaḥīḥ* al-Bukhārī 5402

it lifted the Arabs from *jāhilīyah* (ignorance) into a society with social order and strong political leadership. Its systems gave them the power to control the world from China to Al-Andalus. This pandemic shows us that upholding a wider social order and supporting each other is vital for our survival and success.

The sixth wisdom is to demonstrate to us that there must a higher power that predetermines everything that happens. Allah says, *"Indeed, all things We have created with predestination."*[107] A person might take every single precaution and still be afflicted by the virus, whilst another might walk into the epicentre without being infected. This shows us that everything is in Allah's Hands. The Prophet ﷺ said, *"Caution will not be of any benefit against predestination, but duʿāʾ benefits (matters) that have occurred and that are (yet) to occur. And indeed, duʿāʾ meets with a calamity and fights it until the Day of Judgment."*[108] Even if we take every precaution, what is decreed for us will still happen. This does not mean that we do not take precautions, but rather that we take them with the understanding that they will not prevent what is written for us.

One of the worst plagues that afflicted the early *ummah* was the Plague of Amwās that occurred in Syria in the 18th year of the Hijrah. It is estimated that 50,000 people died. ʿUmar ibn al-Khaṭṭāb was on his way to Syria with reinforcements for the army when he heard that the plague had broken out. They debated about whether or not to continue on the journey until finally, they decided to return to Madīnah. One of the *Ṣaḥābah* objected, saying, *"Are you fleeing from the Decree of Allah?"* To which ʿUmar replied, *"We are fleeing from the Decree of Allah to the Decree of Allah."*[109] Taking precautions is part of Allah's Decree. Allah tells us in the Quran to say, *"Never will we be struck except by what Allah*

107 *al-Qamar* 54: 49
108 Ṭabarānī (33)2/800
109 *Ṣaḥīḥ* al-Bukhārī 5397

has decreed for us; He is our Protector..."[110] We need to etch this ayah into our heart. Nothing will happen to us except what Allah has written. We accept the *qadr* of Allah even as we make *duʿāʾ* for Him to protect us. Trials, like a global pandemic, cause us to remember who is in charge of our affairs, and to turn our hands and our hearts towards Him.

The seventh wisdom that we can observe is that during trials people rediscover their faith. In periods of stress, people who used to neglect their prayers turn back to Allah and this is one of the most blessed pearls of wisdom of any calamity. In the Quran, there are at least a dozen verses in which Allah mentions that in times of difficulty, mankind remembers Him. *"When harm touches man, he invokes Us, lying down on his side, or sitting or standing. But when We have removed harm from him, he passes on his way as if he had never invoked Us for a harm that touched him!"*[111] Allah highlights turning to faith at the time of a calamity, but He never criticises it. The criticism is that after the distress has been lifted, we turn away from worshipping Him. We should increase our *ṣalāh* and *duʿāʾ* during trials, but once the trials have passed, we should not forget the blessings that Allah has bestowed upon us.

We need to remember that the purpose of being tried and tested is to make us turn back to Allah before it is too late. Allah is testing us with a smaller trial to protect us from the larger trial, which is the Hellfire. He says in the Quran, *"What can Allah gain by your punishment, if you are grateful and believe?"*[112] The greatest benefit of a trial such as this pandemic is that we use it to rekindle our relationship with Allah through *ṣalāh* and *duʿāʾ*. We need to remind ourselves that life in this *dunyā* is only temporary, and therefore we need to put our trust in Allah and remain hopeful and

110 *at-Tawbah* 9: 51
111 *Yūnus* 10: 12
112 *an-Nisāʾ* 4: 147

optimistic of a greater reward to come. If we can draw nearer to Allah in this way, then we will have discovered the hidden blessing.

Patience

14

Patience

فَاصْبِرْ إِنَّ وَعْدَ اللَّهِ حَقٌّ

"So be patient.
Verily, the Promise of Allah is true…"

(*ar-Rūm* 30: 60)

Patience is one of the greatest provisions that we have to deal with life's difficulties. This life is a place of tests and trials and every one of us will be tested in different ways. Allah tells us in the Quran, *"O you who believe, seek help through patience and prayer..."*[113] When we are in trouble, or under pressure, these two things will bring us to ease. They will calm us down and help us cope with the problems of this world. Allah says, *"…give glad tidings to those who are patient."*[114] Give them the good news that they will get Paradise and that they are of the fortunate ones.

We are instructed in over ninety verses in the Quran to master the art of patience. Allah says, *"Be patient, as were those of*

113 *al-Baqarah* 2: 153
114 *al-Baqarah* 2: 155

determination among the Messengers..."[115] 'Those of determination' were the *'Ūlū al-'Azm*, the five great prophets – Nuh (Noah), Ibrāhīm (Abraham), Mūsā (Moses), 'Īsā (Jesus) and Muḥammad, peace and blessings of Allah be upon them all. Allah reminds us that one of the primary elements that made these Prophets so great was their characteristic of patience. How do we get willpower and determination? Patience. How do we get fortitude? Patience. True leadership in this world is attained through manifesting patience. If we want to be righteous, we should learn from these great Prophets.

Allah tells us in the Quran that honour and glory come to those nations that have patience. No matter how humiliated they are, if they are patient and understand that there is wisdom in everything, that patience will win over. This understanding is especially important during these difficult times when the *ummah* seems to be humiliated. Allah says, "*...And the good word of your Lord was fulfilled for the Children of Israel because of what they patiently endured...*"[116] Allah tested them, and they responded with patience. Allah says, "*We made from among them leaders, guiding others by Our command, when they were patient...*"[117] He perfected His favours upon the Children of Israel and He made them leaders amongst the people when they demonstrated patience. Look around us at the people who are now considered the pinnacles of human leadership: Gandhi, Martin Luther King and Nelson Mandela. Even without belief is Islam, these were people who made their legacy by displaying patience. If that was the case for them, then how much more so for the one who has patience for the sake of Allah? The one who has patience for the sake of Allah will be raised in ranks in this world as well as in the next, and this is of the blessings of patience.

---

115 *al-'Aḥqāf* 46: 35
116 *al-'A'rāf* 7: 137
117 *al-Sajdah* 32: 24

Allah says in *Sūrah al-ʿAṣr*, *"By time, Indeed, mankind is in loss, Except for those who have believed and done righteous deeds and advised each other to truth and advised each other to patience."* Patience is one of the attributes that prevent us from being in loss. He tells us in *Sūrah ʾĀl ʿImrān* that He loves the *sabirīn*, those who are patient.[118] This is the highest category of blessing: Allah conferring His love for patient people. When Allah loves someone, He is going to help them. He says, *"...Allah is with the patient."*[119] When we demonstrate patience, Allah will love us and be with us in His aid, in responding to our *duʿāʾ*.

Allah mentions in the Quran that those who are patient are amongst those who are guaranteed forgiveness. *"Except for those who are patient and do righteous good deeds, those will have forgiveness and a great reward."*[120] Patience gives us a good ending in this world and guarantees us Paradise in the next. The angels will come from every door of Paradise to welcome and greet those who were patient. Imagine the sight when the believer enters Paradise, all the angels are rushing to greet them. What will they say? The Quran tells us, *"Peace be upon you for what you patiently endured. And excellent is the final home."*[121] Of all of the characteristics that get you into Paradise, the angels are highlighting just one: demonstrating patience.

Patience is one of the few things that Allah will reward without measure. He tells us, *"...the patient will be given their reward without account."*[122] This *ghayri hisāb*, reward without measure, is the same blessing that is given to the act of fasting and it is not a coincidence that patience and fasting have the same reward. Fasting teaches us patience. Patience is essential to success in this world and

118 *ʾĀl ʿImrān* 3: 143
119 *al-Baqarah* 2: 153
120 *Hūd* 11: 11
121 *al-Raʿd* 13: 23-24
122 *al-Zumar* 39: 10

the next. There are many ahadith in which the Prophet ﷺ has told us that on Judgment Day, those who suffer calamities in this world and showed patience, will be rewarded accordingly. He also said, *"If Allah intends good for someone, then he afflicts him with trials."*[123] When Allah loves someone, He tests them. Why? Because these tests are given in order for us to manifest patience.

Ibn Taymiyyah identified three different types of patience:

Patience in the face of a calamity: This is the type of patience that demonstrates our faith at the moment when difficulty strikes. When someone dies, there is a disaster, or when we fall sick, we say only what is pleasing to Allah, we force our thoughts to be positive and we control our emotions. Everybody becomes patient after a week or learns to deal with it after a year, but real patience is demonstrated when we first hear the news. Our Prophet ﷺ said, *"The real patience is at the first stroke of a calamity."*[124]

Patience in withholding from committing sins: The word *ṣabr* (patience), actually comes from the root *ṣabara,* which means 'to restrain or tie-up'. This type of patience is restraining yourself and withholding from acting on what one's heart desires. Things may tempt us, but we control ourselves. This is more difficult than the first type of patience because we have the will to commit the sin, but we have to hold ourselves back. *Ramaḍān* is the perfect example of practising this type of patience, withholding from eating and drinking and committing sins.

Patience in persistence: The highest category of patience is persistence in worship, in doing what is difficult and what has become a routine. Allah tells us, *"...so worship Him and*

123 *Ṣaḥīḥ* al-Bukhārī 5321
124 *Ṣaḥīḥ* al-Bukhārī 1302

have patience for His worship..."[125] Praying five times a day is a sign of manifesting this persistent patience. Allah says, *"Enjoin prayer upon your family, and be patient therein...*"[126] We must always command our family to pray and have persistence and patience in doing it.

Patience is also of levels. Somebody can be patient a little, another in a mediocre fashion and someone else can be patient in an excellent fashion. Allah wants us to strive for perfection. He says, *"So be patient with the most beautiful type of patience.*"[127] The most beautiful type of patience, *ṣabrun jamīl*, is the type we should all strive for. It is the type of patience that entails that other people do not even realise that we are being patient. No one can see that we are frustrated or angry because we have mastered the art of patience so much that only Allah knows how we feel. This is of the perfection of patience. Allah wants quality from us. He tells us, "... *If there are among you twenty who are patient, they will overcome two hundred. And if there are among you one hundred who are patient, they will overcome a thousand...*"[128] Look at the ratios! One person with true patience is equal to ten without.

If we give Allah patience, He promises us true success. When we attain patience, we will get Allah's rewards, His blessings, His forgiveness and His help. So how do we become patient? There are several things that we can do. Firstly, study the blessings of patience. Make ourselves aware of the blessings of patience. We need to read the Quran and hadith that talk about this topic. Imam al-Nawawī has a very good chapter in *Riyāḍ al-Ṣāliḥīn* on the blessings of patience. Simply reading this will make us aware and bring perspective and ease to our situation.

---

125 *Maryam* 19: 65
126 *Ṭā' Hā'* 20: 132
127 *al-Ma'ārij* 70: 5
128 *al-'Anfāl* 8: 65

We also have to train ourselves. Just like we go to the gym to train our body or to the university to train our mind, we need to train ourselves to be patient. *Ramaḍān* is one of the best training grounds; we restrain our *nafs* (self) and do the rituals regularly. Many times, not doing something is actually more difficult than doing it. To control an urge is more difficult than to satisfy it. This is why the mastery of patience is the mastery of faith itself: the two are intertwined. The greater our patience, the greater our faith.

We also need to realise that true patience comes only from Allah. One of His Names is *Aṣ-Ṣabūr*, the One who Demonstrates Infinite Patience. Allah is *Aṣ-Ṣabūr* for many reasons and of them is that He is the source of all patience. The Prophet ﷺ said, *"None is more patient than Allah..."*[129] Allah's servants reject Him, yet He still provides for them. If one person says a word against us, our hearts recoil. People mock and reject Allah and yet still He gives them everything. No being is more patient than Him. Of the meanings of *Aṣ-Ṣabūr* is that He is the One Who Grants Patience to Others, and this is the key. If we want to have patience, we need to make *duʿāʾ* to Allah, use His name *Aṣ-Ṣabūr* and ask Him to give us patience. We need to be eager to seek patience and be determined in striving for it. If we are persistent for the sake of our Lord, then He will grant us patience. Our Prophet ﷺ told us in a beautiful hadith, *"And whoever attempts to be patient will be granted patience by Allah."*[130] We need to remember that Allah just wants to see us try. Once we do that, He will give us patience, and there can be no blessing greater than that.

129 *Ṣaḥīḥ* al-Bukhārī 7378
130 *Ṣaḥīḥ* al-Bukhārī 1469

Arrogance and Humility

15

Arrogance and Humility

عَنِ النَّبِيِّ صلى الله عليه وسلم قَالَ أَلَا أُخْبِرُكُمْ بِأَهْلِ الْجَنَّةِ كُلُّ ضَعِيفٍ مُتَضَعِّفٍ لَوْ أَقْسَمَ عَلَى اللَّهِ لَأَبَرَّهُ أَلَا أُخْبِرُكُمْ بِأَهْلِ النَّارِ كُلُّ عُتُلٍّ جَوَّاظٍ مُسْتَكْبِرٍ

"Shall I not tell you about the Companions of Paradise? They are every humble person considered weak, but if they gave an oath it would be fulfilled. Shall I not tell you about the companions of the Hellfire? They are every harsh, haughty and arrogant person."

(al-Bukhārī 4634)

The first sin ever committed in our history was that of Iblīs. Allah tells us in the Quran that when He created ʾĀdam, Iblīs refused to bow down to him because, "*...he was arrogant...*" and as a result he "*...became amongst the disbelievers.*"[131] Arrogance

131 *Ṣād* 38: 74

is one of the greatest sins of our religion and the verses warning against it are some of the most severe in the Quran. Allah says, "*... those who disdained and were arrogant, He will punish them with a painful punishment...*"[132] He explicitly links the fire of *Jahannam* to arrogance, saying, "It will be said, "Enter the gates of Hell to abide eternally therein, and wretched is the residence of the arrogant."[133] Our Prophet ﷺ said, *"No one will enter Paradise in whose heart is an atom's weight of arrogance."*[134] With warnings as stark as these, it is essential we understand how we protect ourselves from the sin of arrogance, and how we cultivate its cure: humility.

The Prophet ﷺ told us that arrogance is not the love of having beautiful things, rather it is, *"...rejecting the Truth and looking down on people."*[135] It is therefore divided into two categories: arrogance in the *Dīn* and arrogance in the *dunyā*. Arrogance in the *Dīn* is when someone refuses to accept the Truth and this is the type of arrogance that Iblīs had. He knew that he should obey Allah and bow down to ʾĀdam, but he refused to do so. The second type of arrogance is concerning aspects of this *dunyā*. It is when we look down on other people and think ourselves better than them in worldly matters. If we think we are better than someone because of the colour of our skin, we are a racist. And if we think we are better because we have more wealth and privilege, then we are obnoxious. If we see ourselves as better because of the state of our religion, then we do not possess the correct religion, because if we had, we would not be proud. This does not mean that we have to approve of other people's lifestyles. If someone has committed a sin that we did not commit, we should thank Allah, but we should never think ourselves better than them because of it. Allah knows that we all have committed sins in some form throughout our life.

---

132 *an-Nisāʾ* 4: 173
133 *az-Zumar* 39: 72
134 *Sunan* at-Tirmidhī 1999
135 *Ṣaḥīḥ* Muslim 91

The dangers of arrogance are highlighted in a story that the Prophet ﷺ told us about two men. One of them was a drunkard and the other was a worshipper of Allah. Every time the worshipper passed the drunkard, he would tell him to fear Allah and go and pray. One day, the drunkard retorted, and the worshipper became angry saying, *"By Allah! Allah will never forgive you."* The Prophet ﷺ told us that Allah responded, *"Who is he who swore by Me that I will not forgive someone? I have forgiven him and nullified your good deeds."*[136] The drunkard was a sinner but he knew that he was a sinner: he was not arrogant against Allah. The worshipper on the other hand suffered from the sin of arrogance, thinking himself better, and this attitude was a bigger sin in the eyes of Allah than a lifetime of the drunkard's evil.

In *Ṣaḥīḥ Al-Bukhārī* it is recorded that when the Prophet Mūsa, peace be upon him, was asked, *"Who is the most knowledgeable among the people?"* he replied, *"I am the most knowledgeable."* Allah then admonished him revealing, *"A slave among My slaves, at the junction of the two seas, is more knowledgeable than you,"*[137] in reference to Khiḍr. In the story of the Prophet Sulāymān, peace be upon him, we learn that with all the power and blessings that Allah had given him, a whisper came to his heart about his abilities, so Allah sent a small hoopoe bird to remind him, *"…I have encompassed [in knowledge] that which you have not encompassed…"*[138] Sulāymān had control over the wind and the *jinn* and he had a kingdom like no-one else had prior to him, but Allah showed him that this should not allow him to feel superior, even to the smallest bird. Stories such as these demonstrate to us the importance of humility, whatever our worldly position.

136 *Ṣaḥīḥ* Muslim 2621
137 *Ṣaḥīḥ* al-Bukharī 122
138 *an-Naml* 27: 22

At the end of *Sūrah al-Furqān* Allah mentions fifteen characteristics of the people of *Jannah*, the first of which is, "*...those who walk upon the earth in humility...*"[139] Truly humble people are free from the sin of arrogance. The Arabic word for humility is *tawāḍu'*, which comes from *wāḍa* meaning 'to put something down on the ground'. Linguistically, *tawāḍu'* means to lower your ego down. There is a beautiful metaphor for humility in the Quran, in which Allah tells the Prophet ﷺ to, "*...lower your wing to the believers.*"[140] That is why, when people entered the Prophet's *masjid* in Madīnah, they could not tell who was the Prophet ﷺ and who were his followers. Our Prophet ﷺ embodied humility. Anas ibn Mālik told us that when the Prophet ﷺ would enter a room people would not stand up for him because they knew he did not like to be shown outer respect. He was not embarrassed to wear simple clothing or to ride on a donkey. He would be the first to give greetings to the young and old and he would play freely with small children. He intervened to solve marital disputes, attended funerals and regularly visited the sick members of the community. Each of the *Ṣaḥābah* thought that they were the most beloved to the Prophet ﷺ such was his affection for each and every individual. All of this shows us what it means to walk on the earth in humility.

One of the ironies of humility is that it earns the respect of the people. The Prophet ﷺ said, "*Whoever humbles himself by a degree for Allah, glory be to Him, Allah will raise him by a degree. Whoever is arrogant to Allah by a degree, Allah will lower him by a degree, until he is made 'the lowest of the low.'*"[141] Allah will raise the rank of whoever has humility so that they become beloved and respected by others. If we truly have *tawāḍu'* and we eliminate pride from our heart, Allah will write for us the love of the people. When one

139 *al-Furqān* 25: 63
140 *al-Ḥijr* 15: 88
141 *Sunan* Ibn Mājah 4176

is pompous and wants people to look up to him, he ultimately loses their respect. Those who surround him do so because of worldly benefits and as soon as those disappear, they do as well. If we want to be beloved by Allah, the angels and the people, then we need to humble ourselves and consequently, they will all love us.

One of the scholars of the past said that humility is to consider ourselves unworthy of the blessings we have. This does not mean that we do not take advantage of the blessings. If the Prophet ﷺ was given good food or clothes, he utilised them. Rather it is that we thank Allah for His blessings whilst thinking ourselves unworthy of the blessing which has been bestowed upon us. Abū Yazid Al-Bistāmi, a famous gnostic, said, *"Humility is to think of yourself as the most sinful human being on earth."*[142] When we are humble, we think of ourselves as ungrateful, because we recognise all that Allah has given us and know that we cannot thank Him enough. When ʿAbdullāh ibn Mubārak was asked about humility he replied, *"The height of humility is that the one who has less than you should never feel that because you have more you are better. And that the one who has more than you should realise in your presence that he is not better than you."*[143] In other words, when we are interacting with the people, our dignity speaks for our humility.

What are some of the blessings that having humility brings? Humility causes us to count our sins and recognise the blessings of Allah upon us. We cannot truly humble ourselves without recognising that we will never be able to thank Allah for all the blessings that He has bestowed on us. Humility makes us acutely aware of the many sins that we have committed and the need to repent and seek Allah's forgiveness. Humility also leads us to patience and contentment. When we are arrogant, we are always looking to those higher up the ladder, but when we are humble we

142 Ihya Ulum al Din and al Risala al-Qushairiyyah
143 The Book of Humility and Obscurity by Ibn Abi Dunya

are content with what we have. If we remove pride from our heart, we soon realise that we are no better than others. This causes us to cultivate respect and good manners and to control our tongue. In this way, humility leads us towards the blessing of having good *akhlāq* and the Prophet ﷺ told us that, *"Nothing is heavier upon the scale of the believer on the Day of Resurrection than good character."*[144]

If we want to gain the blessings of humility, there are several practical steps that we can take. The first is to gain knowledge. Everything we do in this life should begin with knowledge. Understanding the blessings of humility and the dangers of arrogance as outlined in the Quran and hadith softens our heart and inspires us to action. Next, we need to cultivate *tafakkur* (self-reflection) and *tadabbur* (contemplation). We are the doctor of our own heart and no one can cure our spiritual diseases other than our own self. We need to constantly monitor our symptoms and assess ourselves for the signs of arrogance. We should also participate in activities that others might think beneath us. Our Prophet ﷺ did his own chores; he fetched water, milked animals, patched clothes and mended his own shoes. He was always at the service of the people and actively participated in physical work with the community. He helped to build the *masjid* in Madīnah, passing the bricks until his *thobe* was covered in dust. Before the Battle of the Trench, he joined the Muslims in the trench digging. Through these actions, our beloved Prophet ﷺ displayed both his humanity and his humility, showing us practical ways to earn the pleasure of Allah.

Finally, the most important way to protect ourself from the sin of arrogance is to earnestly make *du'ā'* to Allah that He bestows humility upon us. If we strive to attain humility in our thoughts and actions, Allah will facilitate us, and He will raise us in our

144 *Sunan* at-Tirmidhī 2002

rank because of our efforts. By removing pride from our hearts and lowering our egos for His sake, we will bring ourselves closer to becoming of those who possess the characteristics of the people of *Jannah*.

Forgiveness

16

Forgiveness

وَلْيَعْفُوا وَلْيَصْفَحُوا ۗ أَلَا تُحِبُّونَ أَن يَغْفِرَ اللَّهُ لَكُمْ ۗ
وَاللَّهُ غَفُورٌ رَحِيمٌ

*"…let them pardon and overlook.
Would you not like that Allah should forgive you?
And Allah is Forgiving and Merciful."*

(*an-Nūr* 24: 22)

Forgiveness is one of the most beautiful characteristics of our religion and it runs throughout the Quran and the *Sīrah* of our beloved Prophet Muḥammad ﷺ. Our Prophet ﷺ was sent with the best of character and the noblest manners, and ʿĀʾishah, may Allah be pleased with her, said that, *"He would not respond to an evil deed with an evil deed, but rather he would pardon and overlook."*[145] When we forgive others, we purify our hearts of hatred, jealousy and revenge, but the rewards are far greater than

---
145   *Sunan* at-Tirmidhī 2016

that. Allah tells us, *"And race to a forgiveness from your Lord, and for a Paradise as wide as the heavens and the earth..."*[146] Who are those that earn Allah's forgiveness? Those who, *"...restrain anger and pardon the people."*[147]

One of the most painful episodes in the *Sīrah* was the slander of ʿĀʾishah, may Allah be pleased with her. It is a little-known fact that one of those who spread the slander was her second cousin, Misṭaḥ. To make matters worse, her father was financially supporting him at the time. Imagine how Abū Bakr felt when he heard that a member of his own family was responsible for spreading the rumours. He was so upset that he swore by Allah never to give Misṭaḥ money again. When the situation was eventually resolved, Allah revealed a verse for Abū Bakr that we recite to this day, *"And let not those of virtue among you and wealth swear not to give [aid] to their relatives and the needy and the emigrants for the cause of Allah, and let them pardon and overlook. Would you not like that Allah should forgive you? And Allah is Forgiving and Merciful."*[148] Allah highlighted Misṭaḥ's family ties, the fact that he was a *muhājir* and in need, and enjoined his forgiveness. Allah then tied forgiving him to receiving His own Forgiveness. Abū Bakr heard this verse, made *kaffārah* (expiation) and swore by Allah that he would continue to give *ṣadaqah* to Misṭaḥ for as long as he lived. The lesson from this is clear: if we want Allah to forgive us, we must learn to forgive others.

This example shows us the importance of forgiveness, especially concerning family members. The irony is that we often find forgiveness more difficult with our own flesh and blood. When someone we love hurts us, the pain is more profound, however, because they are members of our family,

146 *Āl ʿImrān* 3: 133
147 *Āl ʿImrān* 3: 134
148 *an-Nūr* 24: 22

we should find it in our hearts to forgive them quicker. Think of the example of the Prophet Yūsuf, peace be upon him. His own brothers threw him into a well and left him for dead. If anyone had the right to exact vengeance, it was him. But after all those years, when the tables were turned and they came to him begging for forgiveness, what did he say? "*...No blame will there be upon you today. Allah will forgive you; and He is the most Merciful of the merciful.*"[149] Yūsuf made it a statement of fact that Allah would forgive them because he himself already had done so. He told his father that it was *Shayṭān* who had created the issues between his brothers and that he did not blame them for what they had done. What a beautiful example of forgiveness we have in the Prophet Yūsuf. Whatever issues we have with our families, they cannot be as bad as this. If the Prophet Yūsuf can forgive, so can we.

Our beloved Prophet Muḥammad ﷺ was the embodiment of forgiveness. There are many instances in the *Sīrah* when he had the opportunity to exact revenge but instead chose to forgive. When the people of Ṭāif rejected and stoned him, Allah sent the angel of the mountains saying, "*O Muḥammad! Order what you wish. If you like, I will let the two mountains fall on them.*" In His wisdom, Allah gave the Prophet ﷺ the opportunity to act on his anger, but before the blood had even dried from his body, he forgave them, saying, "*No, but I hope that Allah will let them beget children who will worship Allah Alone, and will worship none besides Him.*"[150] During the conquest of Makkah, after twenty years of persecution and so many lives lost, the Prophet ﷺ could rightly have taken revenge, but instead, he chose forgiveness, saying "*I will only say to you what Yusuf said to his brothers, 'No blame will there be upon you today'.*

149 *Yūsuf* 12: 92
150 *Ṣaḥīḥ* al-Bukharī 3231

Go, for you are unbound."[151] Even Abū Sufyān, the leader of the Quraysh, praised him at that moment. Our Prophet ﷺ was truly, "*...a mercy to the worlds.*"[152]

The ideal is to forgive and forget, but what if we cannot live up to that ideal? Allah, in His infinite Mercy, has given us a spectrum of possible responses when others wrong us. Whichever of these we choose is permissible, but some are more rewardable than others. At a minimum level, we can return an evil with an evil and we shall not be considered sinful for doing so. This is from the beauty and perfection of our religion. Better than this is to choose not to retaliate but instead to forgive and move on, and this is worthy of a reward. The highest level, which the Prophet ﷺ and Abū Bakr reached, is to forgive and then go further and to reach out in order to resolve any issues that have occurred. Allah says, "*And not equal are the good deed and the bad. Respond with what is better...*"[153] When we reach out to mend broken bonds, we heal the suffering that is in the hearts and strengthen relationships. This is what Allah refers to when He says, "*... thereupon the one whom between you and him is enmity [will become] as though he was a devoted friend.*"[154]

There are two aspects to forgiveness: psychological and spiritual. As for the psychological, we need to realise that when we hold a grudge in our heart, we allow the person to have power over us and we will continue to suffer as a result of the grief and trauma that they have caused. The scholars have said that the one who holds on to anger is like the one holding onto burning coal: he wants to throw it, but he never does, and as a result, he burns his own hand. If we want our heart to heal, we need to forgive and let go. As for the spiritual aspect, know that when we forgive others

151 *Kitāb aṭ-Tabaqāt al-Kabīr* Ibn Saʿd
152 *al-Anbiyā* 21: 107
153 *Fuṣṣilat* 41: 34
154 *Fuṣṣilat* 41: 34

Allah promises to forgive us. When we have it in our heart to show mercy to others, Allah will show mercy to us, and this is far more precious than anything we will gain by seeking revenge.

There is a beautiful narration from the *Sīrah* that highlights the reward of forgiving. One of the *Ṣaḥābah* entered the *masjid* and the Prophet ﷺ said, *"Coming upon you now is a man from the people of Paradise."* He was a man from the *Anṣār* whose beard was dishevelled by the water of ablution. For the next two days, the Prophet ﷺ repeated the same words when the man came in and on the third day, ʿAbdullāh ibn Amr went to stay with the man to see what had earned him that honour. Whenever he went to bed, the man would remember Allah and then rest until he woke for *fajr,* but he did not rise for the night prayer. ʿAbdullāh heard nothing but good words from his mouth, but he did not see anything special about his actions. He asked him, *"O servant of Allah… I heard the Prophet say three times that a man from the people of Paradise was coming to us and then you came. I thought I should stay with you to see what you are doing that I should follow, but I did not see you do anything special. Why did the Prophet speak highly of you?"* The man said, *"I am as you have seen."* When ʿAbdullāh was about to leave, the man said, *"I am as you have seen, except that I do not find animosity in my soul towards the Muslims, and I do not envy anyone because of the good that Allah has given them."* ʿAbdullāh said, *"This is what you have achieved, and it is something we have not accomplished."*[155]

We need to ask ourselves how many grudges are we holding onto in relation to the trivial aspects of this *dunyā*. Now is the time to cleanse our heart, to forgive and let go for the sake of Allah. He tells us, *"Repel, by [means of] what is best, [their] evil…"*[156] If we can respond to harshness with kindness, our actions will bring about

155 *Musnad* Aḥmad 12286
156 *al-Mu'minūn* 23: 96

what is better and earn Allah's reward. The best way to deal with the pain that others have caused is to find a pleasure that is sweeter than our anger, and that pleasure is the worship of Allah. When we taste the sweetness of worship, our pain will dissolve away. On the Day of Judgment, the people with the cleanest hearts will be those closest to the Prophet ﷺ, so we must therefore take this time to forgive, both for this life and the next.

Scholarship

17
Scholarship

اقرأ بِاسمِ رَبِّكَ الَّذي خَلَقَ
خَلَقَ الإِنسانَ مِن عَلَقٍ
اقرأ وَرَبُّكَ الأَكرَمُ
الَّذي عَلَّمَ بِالقَلَمِ
عَلَّمَ الإِنسانَ ما لَم يَعلَم

***"Recite! In the name of your Lord who created,
Created man from a clinging substance,
Read! And your Lord is the most Generous,
Who taught by the pen,
Taught man that which he knew not."***

(*al-ʿĀlāq* 96: 1-5)

Allah began His revelation of the Quran with these five verses. The Angel Jibrīl came to the Prophet ﷺ in the Cave of Hirā, commanding him with the word *iqra*. *Iqra* in the Arabic language has two meanings: to read and to recite. The Prophet ﷺ initially understood it in its first meaning, replying that he did not know how to read. The Angel Jibrīl then squeezed him again until the revelation continued, "*Recite! In the name of your Lord who created,*" clarifying that the command was to recite directly from Allah. A second command then followed, in which the meaning of *iqra* changed to 'read', incorporating all of the knowledge taught to men, "*Read! And your Lord is the most Generous, Who taught by the pen, Taught man that which he knew not.*"[157] Knowledge is therefore of two types: sacred and secular.

Historically, the Muslim *ummah* did not make a distinction between these two types of knowledge. Scholars mastered both Islamic knowledge and secular sciences, and this produced some of the greatest minds in human history. People from all over the globe would look towards the Muslim world for guidance. In medieval Islam, you could not become an *Ālim* until you had studied mathematics. Ibn Taymiyyah studied mathematics, astronomy, biology and medicine before he became a religious scholar, and this formed his understanding as a *faqīh*. Scholars of the past adapted and embraced foreign influences from within the confines of the *Sharīʿah*, and as a result, Islamic civilisation flourished.

Unfortunately, this mindset has not persisted and the past few hundred years has seen a decline in the global relevance of the Islamic scholar. One cause of this is the separation between sacred and secular knowledge. We now have specialists in Islamic sciences and specialists in worldly sciences, but rarely do we have specialists in both. Where previously the two spheres were understood to be complementary to one another, we now find that problems and tensions exist on both sides. Modern curriculums in our Islamic institutions focus on sacred knowledge to the exclusion of all things

157 *al-ʿĀlāq* 96: 1-5

secular. This in turn produces *'Ulemā'* with minimal understanding of worldly sciences, impacting the *fatāwa* they give and the respect they have within the community. Conversely, our *ummah* excels in secular sciences like medicine and engineering, yet often lacks even a basic knowledge of *fiqh*. Experts in worldly fields view religious scholars with disdain and the sad reality is that we no longer view Islamic scholarship as a noble profession that we want our children to aspire to. As a result, we have a crisis of scholarship.

There is no doubt that Islamic scholars have a vital role to play in understanding how we navigate our way in the world; as our Prophet ﷺ said, *"The scholars are the heirs of the Prophets."*[158] But we also have to acknowledge that there are times in our history when our scholars have failed to embrace change. After having been at the cutting edge of civilisation in the 10th to 12th centuries, the Muslim Empire began to fall far behind the advances of Europe. One of the main reasons for this was that when the printing press was invented, Muslim scholars declared it to be *ḥarām*. They had very good scholarly reasons for this position, the primary one being the protection of the classical *ijāzah* system, but they lacked forward-thinking, and failed to see the impact on the development of Muslim society. Ultimately, the printing press did arrive in Muslim lands, but it was not until the 1820s that the first Islamic books were printed in Arabic by Muslims. We have to understand that in our history, some *fatāwā* were designed to protect us from change, but they have in fact held us so far back, that we are still struggling to recover.

This fear of change has also seen mainstream Islamic movements solidify their understanding of Islam. Madrasahs are still teaching students from historical texts that deal with controversies a thousand years old. They continue to look to

158 *Sunan* Abū Dāwūd 3641

the past, whilst modern problems that are much more urgent and challenging, remain unaddressed. The result is that our scholars graduate without appropriate training in how to deal with the realities of the modern world. We are grappling with so many diverse issues, living as minorities in secular humanistic democracies, whilst trying to balance our Islamic responsibilities towards the wider *ummah*. We are residents in nation-states that are engaged in killing Muslims. We are seeing the breakdown of our families and a reversal of social norms. This means that understandings of issues like gender and sexuality, which were historically stable, are now being questioned. We are dealing with the impact of atheism, feminism, liberalism, modernity and democracy. These types of complex tensions did not exist in classical Islam and we will not find the answers in our classical books. Our present situation is unique and we need to recognise those unique problems and call for unique solutions.

When I mention things like this, some people get legitimately concerned about what type of 'unique solutions' I am talking about. They are concerned that I want to change everything including our heritage and our cannons of law. They look to so-called 'progressive Islam', and Muslims who have left their traditional beliefs to embrace a secular way of life and think that I am calling to that. They worry that opening the door slightly will end up opening it all the way and because of this fear, many Muslims just close the doors to any change at all. This is in fact the opposite mistake. We like to think there is 'one Islam' but the fact of the matter is that from the beginning, there have been various interpretations, especially concerning *fiqh*. A simple example of this is in relation to the way we dress. Allah told us that there is an *awrah* for both men and women and wherever Islam went, people took that blueprint and they cut the cloth according to their own cultures. Ibn al-Qayyim said that the *Sunnah* of the Prophet ﷺ was to dress in the clothing of his own people. To follow the *Sunnah,* therefore, we should dress like the people of our own culture. We need to understand that Islam allows for this diversity within the context of the *Sharīʿah.* Scholars need to go back and understand what are the foundations of Islam, and what is allowed to change.

Let me give an analogy to help us understand the situation. Imagine that we are living in our ancestral home. Our house was inherited from our father and he inherited it from his father and so on. We are used to each room and its role, the furniture and the lamps and where they are placed. All of this makes us comfortable because that is how we inherited it. This house represents Islam. But there is a Neighbourhood Housing Committee, and they have some tensions with our house. They want to implement new rules for the houses on their block, some of which seem to be fair, and others of which do not. There are even members of this Committee who think that our house is outdated and needs to be pulled down. This is the Western world. Now imagine that we have a young son. He has grown up in our house and is increasingly uncomfortable with our arrangement. He has seen other people's houses and he wants to change his house. He wants to convert the storage room into a study, he wants to rearrange the furniture and change that old fashioned lamp. We are worried that if we keep on saying 'no' to him, he will get up and leave the house, by which I mean, leave Islam. So we have to reach some type of compromise. We need to preserve the house and make sure our son is still comfortable living with us, whilst making sure that the Neighbourhood Housing Committee does not destroy our house beyond recognition. We need to realise that we can separate the foundations of the house, from its utility. We can separate the structure, from the furniture. Our problem is that most of us do not separate the furniture from the house. We need to educate ourselves about the things in Islam which never change and understand the things which can. We have to make Islam something that is realistic and attainable within the lives that people are currently living. We must find the middle ground and we need to allow for change, where the *Sharīʿah* permits it.

This now raises the question of how do we know which things can change and which things cannot? The easiest way to establish this is when the entire scholarly body of *ʿUlemāʾ* collectively agree on something: this is consensus or *ijmā*. These are the foundations which were revealed by Allah, amongst which are the five pillars of Islam, the six pillars of īmān and the Names and Attributes of Allah. They are all rock solid and can never be altered. There are other things which can be changed, and we need to separate the two. Whilst doing this, we also need to allow for a spectrum of opinion. The early scholars were far more tolerant of diversity than those who claim to follow them today. People have differed since the time of the *Ṣaḥābah* and will continue to do so. The key point to remember is that the opinions should come from scholars, not from people uneducated in Islamic Law, or our desires. We also have to understand that the problems we face are complex and may require multiple specialties, not just one. Salman (ra) said, *"you should give the rights of all those who have a right on you."*[159] This is the key to our solution. Give Islamic scholars their right and give specialists in other fields, be it media, politics or economics the rights that are due to them as well.

The Muslim community in the West has historically suffered from the negative effects of taking their *fatāwā* from overseas. We need to look locally for guidance. The *Sharīʿah* teaches us that the *ʿUlemāʾ* are those that understand the text *and* the context. Ibn al-

159 *Ṣaḥīḥ* al-Bukharī 1968

Qayyim said that half of *fiqh* is understanding the context of the *fatwā* and the person asking the question. A scholar residing in another country may not understand the nuances of our personal situation because there are differences in the minutiae of *fiqh* that occur between time and place. The pros and cons must be weighed concerning each situation and as a result, most *fiqh* involves an understanding of Islam as well as an understanding of the cultural context. It is therefore crucial that we cultivate local *'Ulemā'* who are trained in the foundations of Islam and Islamic Law, but who also have an understanding of the cultures and contexts in which they operate. If a local scholar cannot answer our question, it is their job to ask scholars in other countries, not our job to directly go seeking the answer from scholars elsewhere. Realise that there also has to be an element of experience to gain full wisdom, and it is, therefore, natural that scholars will change their opinions over time.

The Prophet ﷺ told us that, *"The superiority of the learned man over the devout is like that of the moon, on the night when it is full, over the rest of the stars."*[160] Our scholars have a vital role to play in guiding us to the correct path, and we must give them their due. But to be truly guiding lights, our scholars must develop a forward-looking vision for our communities, one that is firmly rooted in Islamic principles, whilst also addressing the complexities of the situations in which we currently live. This will require an understanding of both the sacred and secular sciences, and an understanding of the foundations of Islam and what is allowed to change. It will also need collaboration with experts in other fields, to benefit from the expertise that they provide. These are complex times that we are living in, and forging a vision for the future may appear to be a daunting task, but we must remember that scholars

160 *Sunan* Abū Dāwūd 3641

of the past adapted and embraced new influences as they found them, from within the confines of the *Sharīʿah*, and as a result, Muslim civilisation flourished. Ultimately, the change will happen, and Truth will always prevail.

Unity

18
Unity

وَأَطِيعُوا اللَّهَ وَرَسُولَهُ وَلَا تَنَازَعُوا فَتَفْشَلُوا وَتَذْهَبَ رِيحُكُمْ

"And obey Allah and His Messenger, and do not dispute and [thus] lose courage and [then] your strength would depart…"

(*al-'Anfāl* 8: 46)

Allah has blessed me to travel to many countries in the world and to witness the amazing diversity of this global *ummah*. From Mumbai to New York and London to South Africa, everywhere I find thriving Muslim communities. The Prophet ﷺ said, *"Indeed Allah gathered up the earth for me so that I saw its eastern and western parts, and indeed the dominion of my ummah will reach what was gathered up for me from it."*[161] Our *ummah* spans the globe and our skin colours cover the entire spectrum of humanity. In the midst of all this diversity, what defines us and brings us together? Our faith.

161 *Ṣaḥīḥ* Muslim 2889

In his final sermon, the Prophet ﷺ told us, *"There is no superiority of an Arab over a non-Arab or of a non-Arab over an Arab, or of a red [white] man over a black man, or of a black man over a red [white] man, except in terms of taqwā."*[162] We are all human. We are all children of ʾĀdam, and ʾĀdam was created from dust. No one of us is superior to any other because of our colour, ethnicity or wealth. The only thing that sets us apart in the eyes of Allah is the sincerity of our faith. Even though we know this fundamental teaching to be true, unfortunately, we are all too painfully aware that racism and sectarianism are rife amongst our communities today.

Allah dealt with the topic of breaking into groups in the Quran when He contrasted the success of the Battle of Badr with the failure of Uhud. Concerning Badr, He said, *"...and do not dispute and [thus] lose courage and [then] your strength would depart..."*[163] This was a warning. The *Muhājirūn* and the *Anṣār* put aside their differences and came together for the common good, and their success in battle was as a result of their unity. In contrast, during the Battle of Uhud, there was a dispute between the hypocrites and the *Anṣār* and they split into multiple groups. Allah said of this, *"...until when you lost courage and fell into disputing..."*[164] Inevitably, their disputing led to their demise. When we look at the Muslim world today, we see so many disputes and divides, all of which are weakening us and preventing us from achieving success.

The Prophet ﷺ predicted the dividing of the *ummah* when he said, *"The Jews spilt into seventy-one sects... the Christians split into seventy-two... My ummah will split into seventy-three sects, one of which will be in Paradise and seventy-two in Hell."* It was said, "O Messenger of Allah, who are they?" He said, *"The main body."*[165]

162 *Musnad* Aḥmad 22978
163 *al-ʾAnfāl* 8: 46
164 *ʾĀl ʿImrān* 3: 152
165 *Sunan* Ibn Majah 3992

Many scholars of the past took this hadith literally and tried to identify each of the sects, but every time they did so, new groups would emerge. The stronger opinion is that this is an Arabic expression meaning 'many groups'. The point of the hadith is that our *ummah* will divide into more groups than any of the other religions, and this is because it will survive for the longest period.

How do we understand the fact that the Prophet's statement appears to indicate that a large proportion of the *ummah* will be misguided and go to Hell? He said that the rightly guided group was 'the main body', or the masses. Seventy-two out of seventy-three is a large fraction only if all the parts are the same size. To claim that this hadith indicates that the bulk of the *ummah* is misguided is grossly inaccurate. The reality is that the majority of rejected groups are very small. The Prophet ﷺ said, *"My ummah will split…."*, indicating that every one of those seventy-three groups is in fact a part of his community. The issue is that they did something to cause them to break away from the main body of Muslims. He used the word *iftirāq* meaning a cleaving or breaking away, and not *ikhtilāf* meaning a difference of opinion. The majority of scholars agree that this refers to fundamental differences of theology, not merely differences of the legal position. Different *fiqh* opinions are legitimate and tolerated from within the fold of Islam. It is only ignorant people who make these issues bigger than they need to be. That is not to say that every difference can be accepted and tolerated. Some views are clearly aberrant deviations from the Truth, and some may even expel a person from Islam. But that is a decision for qualified scholars to make, and there is a time, place and language for such discussions. This hadith, unfortunately, has a long history of being misunderstood and misused for the justification of splitting the *ummah*. The fact is that from the earliest generations, the *ummah* has had differences of opinion, but they did not allow this to lead them to separation. Allah commands us in the Quran, *"Hold firmly to the rope of Allah, all together, and do not become divided..."*[166] A difference of opinion should not lead to a difference in the heart.

The problem with sectarianism is that it has made our allegiances to books written by men rather than to the Quran and *Sunnah*. In order to be trained as an Ālim, you have to go through a school, and each school is eager to protect its own interests by demonstrating how correct it is. They do this by separating themselves from the other schools of thought, and students come out making disparaging remarks about other groups. The result is that we literally have one group of Muslims hating another group of Muslims because of these allegiance issues and this is devastating our community. People think that the Truth can only come from their strand of Islam, and some scholars revel in promoting differences and sectarianism. But we need to understand that Islam is above any of these man-made movements and move away from the mindset of trying to divide practising Muslims.

Our main focus should not be on criticising others, because our faith commands us to love our fellow Muslims. *"None of you will have faith until he loves for his brother what he loves for himself."*[167] This is the Golden Rule and every Prophet taught it. Sometimes we do not like differences, but these differences will continue to exist regardless. Stereotyping and stigmatising are un-Islamic and can lead to hatred, which can then lead to violence, as we know all too well. A famous scholar of hadith, Ibrāhim ibn ʿAbdullāh ibn al-Ḥasan (d. 145 AH), lived through a time when the Muslim world began to splinter up into different sects and groups. When he was asked about the beliefs of another group, he said, *"Come, help me (to unite) in what all of us have agreed about, and then once we have done that, let's discuss the differences!"*[168] People

166 *ʾĀl ʿImrān* 3: 103
167 *Ṣaḥīḥ* al-Bukharī 13
168 Al-Awasim wal Qawasim

may have different interpretations of Islam, but as long as they believe in the *kalimah*, and all the things necessitated by that belief, then they are Muslims and they deserve our respect. We all share the same core beliefs: love of Allah and worship of Him, respect for the Messenger and following his *Sunnah*, love for the *Ṣaḥābah,* and belief in the five pillars of Islam and the six pillars of īmān. These are the things that we can all unite upon.

If we want Allah to love us, then we must learn to love each other. Allah tells us in a beautiful *hadith qudsī*, *"My love is due for those who love one another for My sake; My love is due for those who visit one another for My sake; My love is due for those who help one another for My sake; My love is due for those whose hearts are free of grudges and who uphold ties with one another for My sake."*[169] This shows us that with the right intention, overcoming our differences and strengthening the bonds of brotherhood can enable us to gain the ultimate reward: the love of Allah. The root of the word for brotherhood actually means 'to intend good for somebody' and our brother is called our brother because we want nothing but good for him. This concept in the Quran applies not just to blood brothers, but also people of the same tribe or ethnicity and widens out even further to include all members of the *ummah*. In fact, Allah tells us that, *"The believers are [nothing other than] brothers..."*[170] How then can we strengthen this concept of brotherhood within our hearts? The hadith tells us. Visit one another for the sake of Allah and strive to help those who are experiencing difficulty. Uphold the ties of kinship, learn to forgive our brother in Islam and do not allow ourselves to hold grudges. Our heart will become lighter and we will draw closer to Allah as a result.

The concept of loving one another for the sake of Allah is beautifully illustrated in an incident that took place around thirty

169 *Musnad* Aḥmad 21575
170 *al-Ḥujurāt* 49: 10

years after the *Hijrah*. A young man named Abū Idrīs Al-Khawlānī went to study Islam in the Muslim capital at that time, Damascus. He entered the central *masjid* and saw a man teaching there with people gathered around him, listening in humility and awe. Abū Idrīs asked, 'Who is this?' The man next to him replied, 'Don't you know? This is Muʿādh Ibn Jabal.' He was one of the great scholars of the *Ṣaḥābah* and despite his young age, he was the *faqih*. A love for Muʿādh entered the heart of Abū Idrīs and he decided that he would study under him. He told himself that the next day he would be the first in the *masjid* so that he could talk to Muʿādh alone. He entered the *masjid* in the middle of the night and found Muʿādh already there praying. Abū Idrīs gave him *salam* and told him that he loved him for the sake of Allah. When Muʿādh heard this, he held onto Abū Idrīs' collar, dragged him close, and said, 'Did you swear by Allah that you have a love for me just because of Allah?' Abū Idrīs said, 'I swear by Allah.' Muʿādh then said, 'If what you say is true, let me tell what my ears heard directly from the Prophet ﷺ. I heard him say, that Allah Almighty said, *"Those who love each other for the sake of My Glory will be upon pulpits of light, admired by the prophets and martyrs."*[171]

Let this be a source of inspiration for us to strive harder to cultivate a sense of brotherhood and unity within this *ummah*. It is Allah's blessing upon us that we are a richly diverse community, and we need to remember the lessons from the *Sīrah* about not dividing or breaking into groups. We should keep our focus on the many things that unite us, rather than dwelling on differences. Unity does not have to mean uniformity; we can have differences of opinion, but let us do it privately and with mutual love and respect. We need to avoid scholars and groups who promote division and sectarianism and seek out those who encourage unity in the *ummah*. Ultimately, our God is One, our Prophet ﷺ is one,

171 *Sunan* at-Tirmidhī 2390

our Book is one and our *qiblah* is one. Let us unite on this shared understanding in order to strengthen our *ummah*. If we can love one another for the sake of Allah, Allah promises that He will love us and what more blessed thing could we strive for than the love of Allah?

Spouses

19
Spouses

وَمِن آياتِهِ أَن خَلَقَ لَكُم مِن أَنفُسِكُم أَزواجًا لِتَسكُنوا إِلَيها

"Of His Signs, is that He created for you from yourselves mates, that you may find tranquillity in them..."

(*ar-Rūm* 30: 21)

Allah, in His infinite wisdom, created us in pairs. Knowing our needs, Allah created spouses for us in the most intimate way, to bring us peace and security. It is because of this that the Prophet ﷺ told us that one of the greatest blessings we can have in this world, is a righteous spouse. Allah says, "*...They are garments for you, and you are garments for them...*"[172] Like clothing, spouses cover and protect us, helping us to adapt to the circumstances we are living in. Their companionship enables us to bear the hardships and discomforts of this *dunyā,* as well as enhancing the blessings of the Hereafter. When Allah created 'Ādam, He made Hawā as his wife,

172 *al-Baqarah* 2: 187

before entering them both into *Jannah*. Allah knew, that without a righteous spouse, even Paradise could not be fully enjoyed.

Allah tells us that spouses will *"...find tranquillity..."*[173] in each other and we see this beautifully illustrated in the *Sīrah* of the Prophet ﷺ. When the Prophet ﷺ became afraid after receiving the first revelation, it was his wife Khadījah, may Allah be pleased with her, that he ran to for comfort and reassurance. ʿĀʾishah, may Allah be pleased with her, told us that when the Prophet ﷺ was with her in their home, he would intimately display his love and affection by reclining in her lap. He was the embodiment of gentleness with his wives, and he enjoined other men to be the same also, saying, "The best of you are those who are the best to their wives. And I am the best of you to my wives."[174]

Allah says of spouses that we should, *"...live with them in kindness..."*[175] The word translated as kindness here is *maʾrūf*, which incorporates the best of manners according to the time and culture that we are living in. People look at the rights of the husband and wife in the books of Islamic Law as marital guidance, but these books cannot teach us the etiquettes and norms of a society. We should strive to be the best spouse that we can be, based on our society and times.

In Arabic, there are many words for love, and when Allah says, *"...He has put between you affection and mercy..."*[176] He uses the word *mawadda,* implying a love that is gentle and full of compassion. This type of love that Allah has placed in the hearts of spouses is different from romantic love, which is temporary in nature. *Muwadda* is a love that causes us to care so deeply about our spouse that we are prepared to sacrifice our happiness for

173 *ar-Rūm* 30: 21
174 *Sunan* Ibn Mājah 1977
175 *an-Nisāʾ* 4: 19
176 *ar-Rūm* 30:21

theirs. It is a love that develops throughout marriage and remains strong after ten or twenty years. It is truly a miracle of Allah that He bestows this love on two people, who were once strangers, and through it they become inseparable.

Of course, marriage is not just about love: it is about sacrifice and commitment and above all forgiveness. In a verse addressing spouses, Allah says, *"...But if you pardon and overlook and forgive, then indeed, Allah is Forgiving and Merciful."*[177] Forgiveness is the key to marital harmony. If we hold onto grudges and keep returning to past events, we will never be able to find peace. When marital issues arise, people tend to overlook the positive aspects and focus on the negative, but the Prophet ﷺ told us that we should turn our attention to what pleases us in our spouse. No doubt they will have certain characteristics that are irritating for us, just as we have aspects that will be irritating to them but we must learn to overlook and forgive. There are so many things we can find to be grateful for.

All marriages will have some type of conflict, and even our beloved Prophet ﷺ experienced this. When a problem occurs, many couples end up arguing, but we need to control ourselves in the heat of the moment and come back to the issue when we have both calmed down. The Prophet ﷺ told us, *"If one of you is angry while he is standing, let him sit down so his anger will leave him; otherwise, let him lie down."*[178] He also advised us to seek refuge from *Shayṭān* and to make *wuḍū*. When the Prophet ﷺ was angry, people could see it in his face, but they never heard it from his tongue. A scholar of the past said, *"Speech is like an arrow that you shoot. Once you shoot it, you cannot bring it back. So be careful what arrows you shoot."*[179] No-one will get upset with us for being angry,

177 *at-Taghābun* 64: 14
178 *Sunan* Abū Dāwūd 4782
179 Al-Risalah al-Mughniyya by Ibn al-Binaa

but everyone will get upset about what we said in the state of anger. Remember that the goal is not to win the argument; it is to save the marriage. If we can learn to control ourselves, we are promised a magnificent reward. Our Prophet ﷺ told us, *"I guarantee a house on Jannah for the one who gives up arguing..."*[180]

Clear communication is a vital part of maintaining a healthy relationship. As Khalil Gibran said, *"Between what is said and not meant, and what is meant and not said, most of love is lost."* Psychologists tell us that if we want to resolve a problem, we need to communicate using explicit phrases. We need to state our issue in simple terms, from our perspective. We should not use accusative language, saying, 'You did this wrong', because it only makes our spouse feel defensive. Rather, we should speak in the first person and say, 'I felt this way'. Often, we are guilty of making assumptions about what our spouse is thinking or feeling. It might be that they did not understand the severity of what they did or said and understanding how it made us feel will have an impact on them. We should also think carefully about the issues that we choose to raise, prioritising important points and letting smaller things go by.

If the problem cannot be solved between the couple the Quran mentions another step. Each spouse should reach out to someone they look up to in their family, someone who has wisdom and can arbitrate in the dispute. All too often we are blinded by our worldview and bringing in a third party can give us a fresh perspective. Each arbitrator should meet with the husband and wife separately, consider the issues, and then come together to find the best way forward. Hearing someone we look up to advise us about what we need to rectify can sometimes be enough to make us realise the errors of our ways. One of the most optimistic verses

180 *Sunan* Abū Dāwūd 4800

in the Quran about difficulties in marriage is, *"...if they both desire reconciliation, Allah will cause it between them..."*[181] If both spouses are sincere and want to reconcile, Allah promises to bring their hearts together. Never underestimate the power of *duʿāʾ* in this respect. If we are supposed to make *duʿāʾ* for unity amongst people we do not even know, then how much more so for the sake of our marriage? We need to constantly ask Allah to soften our hearts and bring us together.

If the differences between the couple are found to be irreconcilable, then they may divorce as a last resort. This should only be pursued after all other avenues have been exhausted, and *Istikhārah* (prayer for guidance) has been prayed. Unfortunately, divorce has become such a taboo in our communities that most people do not know how to go about it in the proper Islamic way. Divorce should never be done in haste. Like marriage, it has specific *fiqh* rulings, and we need to be aware of these in case this situation arises. Allah says, *"...divorce them at their prescribed periods, and count (accurately)."*[182] Divorce should not be initiated when a woman is on her menses, or if there have been any intimate relations between the couple within the last month. This is designed to prohibit heat of the moment decision-making and to give the couple time to fully consider the consequences of their actions. Even once the first *ṭalāq* has been uttered, if no abuse is taking place, the couple should continue to cohabit for three consecutive menstrual cycles in order to give them time to reconcile. If *ṭalāq* process continues with no avail after further attempts of reconciliation, then they should part amicably. Allah even says that the husband should give the wife a parting gift.

The *Sharīʿah* has so many steps in place to preserve the marriage, and if we followed them, many of the divorces that we

181 *an-Nisāʾ* 4: 35
182 *aṭ-Ṭalāq* 65: 1

see today could be averted. But it is important to remember that even if a marriage does end, it does not mean that the couple is not righteous. We can have the best īmān and the best *taqwā* and the marriage still might not work. This should not prohibit us from marrying again. At the time of the Prophet ﷺ, there was no stigma in marrying someone who was divorced. Some of the greatest *Ṣaḥābah* and several of the Mothers of the Believers were divorcees. The shame that we have attached to it, in particular by blaming divorce on women, is simply un-Islamic.

If we want to preserve our marriage, the most important thing that we can do is to not take our spouse for granted. We should beautify ourselves, smile, and make sure we take time to appreciate them every single day. Further, we should complement our spouse in private and in public and this will create positive feelings between the couple. We should also prioritise spending quality time together as a couple, even if we schedule it in just before bed because life is busy. Talk to each other; share our feelings, goals and fears. We should not trivialise the daily chores that we do together because they provide the framework for a healthy family life. We should make mealtimes a shared event where everyone plays a part, this will create a sense of intimacy and build trust between family members. We should try and make time every week or so to spend time alone together away from the children. Once a year, take a vacation or some time out to reconnect and reflect. If we can establish these things, we will reap the rewards of the renewed sense of closeness that they bring.

We should know that our relationship with our spouse and how we live our Islam in our household will be the main factor that preserves Islam in our family. We embody Islam in the eyes of our children and if we cannot live by its teachings, they will think that the religion itself has failed. If our home is a place of harshness and conflict, our children will associate this with the faith and end up rejecting Islam. However, if we strive to practice Islam and we fill our home with love and forgiveness, our children will be inspired to preserve the faith for the generations to come. We will protect Islam through our family and we will protect our family through Islam. We make *duʿāʾ* for Allah to bless us with a righteous spouse, who will help us to establish a righteous family, at the heart of a righteous community and who will be our companion by the rivers of *Jannah Al-Firdous.*

Next Generation

20

Next Generation

رَبَّنَا وَاجْعَلْنَا مُسْلِمَيْنِ لَكَ وَمِن ذُرِّيَّتِنَا أُمَّةً مُّسْلِمَةً لَّكَ

"Our Lord, and make us Muslims [in submission] to You and from our descendants a Muslim nation [in submission] to You..."

(*al-Baqarah* 2: 128)

Allah tells us many inspiring stories about young people in the Quran. Think of the Prophet Ibrāhīm, peace be upon him, destroying the idols and risking the wrath of his people when he was still just a boy. Or the People of the Cave; the young men who sought refuge from their society in order to worship Allah alone. Allah tells us that, *"No one believed in Mūsa, except [some] youths among his people..."*[183] and we learn from the *Sīrah* that it was the young people of Makkah who readily accepted Islam. Young people have the ability to ask questions of their societies, the conviction to follow their beliefs with action and the sincerity not to be afraid.

183 *Yūnus* 10: 83

These are amongst the reasons why, on the Day of Resurrection, Allah will bless the young person who grows up in His worship, with the honour of being in His Shade.

We all want our children to have the conviction of these youths, to know what they believe in and stand up for what is right. However, modernity is upon us like a fast-flowing river, bringing changes so rapid it can feel hard to keep up. Globalisation, technology and entertainment are permeating our societies, and the rise of atheism and ever-changing social norms mean that our young people are facing challenges unprecedented in the history of our *ummah*. Muslim youth living in the West feel caught between the values of their parents and the values of the societies they are living in. Their families often do not understand the problems they face and as a result, many of our young people are left feeling isolated and confused. This has led to a spiritual crisis amongst the next generation of Muslims, and not addressing it is having devastating consequences.

What can we do in the face of these challenges? Firstly, we need to go back to the foundations. The three most common questions I get asked by young people are: 'How do I know that there is a Creator?', 'How do I know that Islam is the correct religion?' and then, 'Why is Islam so restrictive?' Questions about the existence of God can make us uncomfortable as Muslim parents, but they starkly illustrate the spiritual state of our youth and unless we address them, their faith will never be firm.

The most obvious answer to the question of, 'How do I know that there is a Creator?' is the creation itself. Look at the finely balanced systems that sustain our life on earth. When we study biology, chemistry or physics we see harmony in creation: everything has a purpose and fits perfectly into place. If we were walking in the desert and found a perfectly formed circle of rocks, would we think that they had landed that way by accident? Our first thought would be that someone has placed them there with a purpose because we know that design does not happen by chance. We live with this understanding of cause and effect: if there is an effect then something must have caused it. Then how about life itself? If we are truly just animals, where do mercy and morality come from? They have no place in Darwinian evolutionary theory and yet they clearly exist. Allah is *Ar-Raḥmān*, the Merciful, and He placed within us mercy. Why else do we have the instinct to care for the weak? What about morality? Where does this innate sense of 'right' and 'wrong' come from? Why do we have a yearning for justice if all of life is without purpose? The psychological and moral aspects of the human being are what distinguish us from the animals and show us that our human condition speaks of more than just chance. It is for this reason that religion has been so enduring throughout the ages. Allah says, *"And We created not the heavens and the earth and all that is in-between them without purpose!"*[184] He made us with the *fiṭrah*, the natural disposition to understand His existence and the desire to worship Him. Our purpose is found in His worship.

The next question young people ask is, 'How do I know that Islam is the correct religion?' Many of us have never even considered this question, but for our youth, the situation is very different. What makes them know that Islam is right? If we accept that there is one All-Powerful Creator God, then we have to ask, 'How do we worship Him?' We can only know the answer to this question through Revelation. Allah has guided Prophets from the beginning of time to call people to His worship, but only His final Revelation remains preserved: the Quran. It is the direct Word of God and we can read it just as it was revealed: it is truly an eternal miracle. This combined with the preserved *Sunnah* of the Prophet

---

184 *Ṣād* 38: 27

Muḥammad ﷺ provides us with the blueprint for how to live our lives. From how to wash, pray, raise our families and care for the poor, Islam is a complete way of life that brings morality and justice to society. All of this speaks of the guidance of a Creator, God who knows us intimately, and a universal Divine model for how to live the best life. As Allah says, *"O mankind! There has come to you instruction from your Lord and healing for what is in the breasts and a guidance and mercy for the believers."*[185]

If it is the right religion, then 'Why is Islam so restrictive?' In a day and age when almost anything goes in terms of satisfying our desires, the boundaries that Islam puts in place can appear constricting: no drugs or alcohol, no sex before marriage and modesty in dress. We need to understand that our Creator made these guidelines for our protection because He knows us better than we know ourselves. Allah tells us that He, *"...makes lawful for them the good things and prohibits for them the evil."*[186] He knows what will harm us and because of this, He gave us these prohibitions. The objectives of Islamic law are to protect religion, life, intellect, family and wealth, and for these rights to be preserved within society, prohibitions and restrictions must be in place. Allah is *Al-Ḥakīm*, the All-Wise, and all of His Laws have wisdom. They are timeless and universal; they bring about justice and demonstrate a higher calling for man. He says, *"...Allah does not intend to make difficulty for you, but He intends to purify you..."*[187] These restrictions are not meant to bring us hardship, they are meant to purify us and facilitate the path to His worship.

Asking questions with the right intention has never been forbidden in our religion: even the angels asked. We should encourage our young people to ask questions and be open in our

185 *Yūnus* 10: 57
186 *adh Dhāriyāt* 7: 157
187 *al-Mā'idah* 5: 6

discussions. Pushing them away or chastising them will only fuel their doubts or lead them towards the other end of the spectrum: radicalisation. Radicalisation amongst our youth is a topic that many in our community find difficult to speak about, but one that also needs to be addressed. Our young people feel legitimate anger at the treatment they see of Muslims around the world and many of our clerics are so apolitical that these topics are never spoken about in the *masājid*. This causes our youth to go underground or online where they hear radical voices that speak to their concerns. We all know that the root cause of 'Islamic terrorism' is often legitimate political grievances, but the question is not whether or not injustice exists, it is what we as Muslims living in other parts of the world do about it. In order to fight against injustice and oppression, the methods we use must be the most effective and Islamically legitimate; both things need to be taken into account. It is right to be angry, but our anger should not lead us towards more injustice: militancy will only make matters worse. We see again and again how the young people who become involved with these movements have minimal knowledge of Islam. They do not have the wisdom to understand correct motivation and action, or the ability to see that the methods these people call to are fundamentally wrong. For Muslims living in Western lands, the best way that we can fight against injustice is with the tongue and with the pen.

To respond effectively to the concerns of our young people, we need to have more scholars who were born, raised and trained in the countries they are living in. The first immigrant generation had no choice but to bring their *imāms* from back home, but it has been more than fifty years and we need to begin preparing for the future. If we want Islam to flourish, our leaders must come from amongst us and we must encourage our youth to deepen their Islamic knowledge in order to prepare. We need locally trained *imāms* as well as a grass-roots movement of young people

Islamically educated in the West. Our communities need both male and female *ʿUlemā* if they are going to thrive. Islam has always had female scholars, ʿĀʾishah, may Allah be pleased with her, being the most well-known amongst them, but there were also the *Muḥaddithāt* (female scholars of hadith) and those who taught our famous scholars such as Imam Bukhārī and Ibn Taymiyyah. When we deprive women of Islamic education, we lose a vital lifeline in our communities, and we need to revive this heritage if we want Islam to survive.

The crisis we are witnessing amongst our youth results from the fact that we prioritised the pursuit of the *dunyā* over the *Dīn*, but our love for our children must transcend this secular world. Ibn al-Qayyim said, *"How many parents have caused misery to their offspring in this world and the Hereafter; by neglecting them, and by not disciplining them and helping them to his lusts?"*[188] We have neglected to give our youth proper Islamic *tarbiyah* and this has left them immature and unprepared. If we want the next generation to be ready to take responsibility for this *ummah*, we need to begin treating them as adults, because if we continue to treat them like kids, they will never grow up. Previous generations prioritised this type of character building and we see this in examples of Usāma bin Zayd who lead the Muslim army when he was barely out of his teens. Think of the conversation between the Prophet Ibrahīm, peace be upon him, and his son Ismāʿīl, after he saw him in a dream, *"...O my son, indeed I have seen in a dream that I [must] sacrifice you, so see what you think..."*[189] Ibrahīm consulted his son like an adult, engaging him in an intellectual conversation and seeking his advice. This is the essence of *tarbiyah*. We need to educate our youth, give them responsibility and consult them; only then will they be strong enough to rise to the challenges they face.

188 *Tuhfat Al-Maudūd Bi-Ahkām Al-Maulūd* Ibn Qayyim
189 *aṣ-Ṣāffāt* 37: 102

Inherent in this is that we must also lead by example: if we want our children to be firm upon the *Dīn*, then we must also be firm ourselves.

Never underestimate the power of *duʿāʾ* when it comes to your children. We need to constantly make *duʿāʾ* that they will serve this *ummah* and humanity at large and be successful in both this world and the next. Remember the *duʿāʾ* of Ibrahīm when he was laying the foundations of the Kaʿbah in the deserted valley of Makkah, *"Our Lord, and make us Muslims [in submission] to You and from our descendants a Muslim nation [in submission] to You..."*[190] Allah heard his *duʿāʾ* and look at the result!

190 *al-Baqarah* 2: 128

Legacy

21
Legacy

وَاجعَل لي لِسانَ صِدقٍ فِي الآخِرينَ

"And grant me a reputation of honour among later generations."

(*ash-Shuʿarāʾ* 26: 84)

The desire to be a good role model and leave a positive legacy is something that we are instructed to make *duʿāʾ* for in the Quran. At the end of *Sūrah al-Furqān*, Allah tells us to ask, *"Our Lord, grant us from among our wives and offspring comfort to our eyes and make us an example for the righteous."*[191] Ibn Al-Qayyim highlighted the importance of intention in relation to this *duʿāʾ* because there is a difference between desiring a legacy for fame and desiring it for the sake of Allah. We do not seek a legacy for the sake of our ego, but rather because we want Allah to be exalted through the inspiration we provide to others.

191 *al-Furqān* 25: 74

To understand how we can leave a legacy, we need to look at the impact we can have, given our talents. We should not judge our weaknesses in the light of the strengths of others, Allah uniquely created us and we all have a different role to play. Look at the *Ṣaḥābah* and how varied they were. Khālid Ibn Walīd, was a great warrior, but he was not known for narrating hadith, and Ḥassān ibn Thābit was a gifted poet, but he could not fight. No one role is more important than any other; the *ummah* needs people in each and every field. We need to ask ourselves what are we able to do based on our skills and resources. How far and how long the consequences of our actions will reach is something that only Allah knows.

Think of our great *ʿUlemāʾ* and the legacies they left behind. Imām al-Bukhārī lived for just over sixty years, an average lifespan, but more than a thousand years later his legacy still thrives. The compilation of his *Ṣaḥīḥ* was the culmination of years of exhaustive research and his sincerity was such that he would not record a hadith until he had made *wuḍū* and performed two *rakaʿāt* of prayer. Allah accepted this from him and to this day we cannot give a *khuṭbah* or Islamic talk without mentioning his name. Through sincere intention and dedication to his goal, Imam al-Bukhārī created a legacy that will earn him rewards until the Day of Judgment. Let us reflect on that for a moment.

What can we do to nurture our legacy? We need to begin by seeking knowledge. By knowing how our religion and the benefits of different actions leads us to have higher goals. We need to learn how much Allah praises those who do good deeds, and this will intensify our desire to strive to earn those rewards. Remember that actions are distinguished by the sincerity of intention and the reward of even small deeds can be infinitely multiplied.

Next, we need to find good role models, people that we can look up to. We should always strive to be like those who are above us in *Dīn*. Our Prophet ﷺ told us that when it comes to matters of the religion, we should look to those above us, but in matters of the *dunyā,* we should look to those below us, as this will ensure that we are thankful for what we have. Sadly, most of us do the opposite. We look to those below us in *Dīn* and get the false sense that we are doing well, but when it comes to matters of the *dunyā,* we are constantly looking to those above us and thinking that we do not have enough. If our role models are people who only seek the pleasures of this world, what do we think our end will be? We need to identify positive Islamic role models; people who are striving for the rewards of the Hereafter. We should study the life of the Prophet ﷺ and the *Ṣaḥābah* and those who are striving to follow in their path and take them as our inspiration.

Furthermore, we need to know the importance of good companionship and look closely at who our friends are. The Prophet ﷺ told us, *"A man is upon the religion of his best friend, so let one of you look at who he befriends."*[192] We need to be around people who have high aspirations, those who are proactive and encouraging. Not setting high expectations and goals is one of the plots of *Shayṭān*. If the people around us are holding us back, we need to move away from them. We only have one life to live and we need to do our utmost not to waste it. Ibn Abbās, may Allah be pleased with him, was only thirteen years old when the Prophet ﷺ passed away. He had a close friend who he asked to join him in learning ahadith from the *Ṣaḥābah*, but his friend scoffed at him saying he just a child. Ibn Abbās cut the friend off and started studying. He would wait outside the houses of the *Ṣaḥābah* for hours in the desert heat, just to ask about one hadith. Then he would go and be in their service so that he had the opportunity

192 *Sunan* at-Tirmidhī 2378

to ask more. As he grew to become an adult, the *Ṣaḥābah* slowly began to die, and the knowledge that he had accumulated was such that people from all over the world would come to learn from him. When his old friend saw Ibn Abbās teaching others he said, *"You were smarter than me."*[193] Companionship is everything.

We need to always aim high. We learn from the *Sīrah* that before the Battle of Tabūk, some Muslims were unable to join the army because they could not afford an animal to carry them on the journey and they became deeply distressed. Allah revealed, *"Nor [is there blame] upon those who, when they came to you that you might give them mounts, you said, "I can find nothing for you to ride upon." They turned back while their eyes were overflowed with tears of grief that they could not find something to spend [for the cause of Allah]."*[194] Our Prophet ﷺ told us that because of the sincerity of their intention, they were rewarded as if they had participated in the battle. This illustrates the importance of aiming high: even if we do not reach the top, we might be rewarded as if we had.

To create a lasting legacy, we must also be proactive. Look at the earliest revelation of Quran, when Allah appointed the Prophet ﷺ as a Messenger. He told him, *"O you who covers himself, Arise and warn."*[195] It feels good to be safe and covered, but we must get up and act. Allah commands us to do good deeds and strive for His Mercy with verbs like '*flee*', '*run to*' and '*win the race*'. The reality is that most of us have a stronger desire to win the race of this world, rather than the race for the Hereafter. We compete for the *dunyā* the way the *Ṣaḥābah* competed for the *Ākhirah*, but we should always remind ourselves of our ultimate goal. We need to make a plan for what we want to achieve, then strive for it, and always make *Jannah* our primary aim.

193 al-Darimi 1/150 (570), al-Tabarani (10/244) (10614)
194 *at-Tawbah* 9: 92
195 *al-Muddathir* 74: 1-2

Remember that even the smallest actions with the right intention can have long-lasting effects. If we change just one person's life, it could have results far greater than we can imagine. A beautiful example of this occurred just before the migration to Madīnah. In the last phases of the Prophet's ﷺ time in Makkah, the persecution became so intense that he knew he would soon have to leave. He started approaching the largest and most powerful tribes to get support. During the days of *Hajj*, as he was making his way between two tribes in Mina, he saw a small group of five people. He approached them to ask who they were, and they said they were from the tribe of Khazraj in Yathrib. The Prophet ﷺ had barely even heard of this tribe, but he decided to sit with them and share the call to Islam. Those five people went back and began preaching to their tribe and the next year seventy people came back as Muslims. The year after that, they were so strong in numbers that they offered the Prophet ﷺ refuge in what is now known as the city of Madīnah. The small seed of Islam that was planted in the hearts of those people quite literally changed the course of history.

Lastly, I want to share some inspiration that I got from my teacher while I was studying in Madīnah. He narrated the hadith of the Prophet, *"At the beginning of every century Allah will send to this ummah someone who will renew its religious understanding."*[196] and asked the class, 'You all know this hadith, don't you?' We said that we did. He asked, 'What's the question that everybody has on their minds?' We answered, 'Who is the reviver of our times?' The Shaykh replied, 'That's your mistake. You've already accepted that someone else will get to the top. Why don't you make *duʿāʾ* to Allah, 'O Allah! Make me the reviver who's going to come at the end of every hundred years.' Somebody has to play that role, why not you?'

196 *Sunan* Abū Dawūd 4291

We should not be afraid to aim for the top. If we set ourselves a high goal and spend our lives striving for it, by the time we die, we will have earned innumerable rewards. Allah says, *"And those who strive for Us, We will surely guide them to Our ways. And indeed, Allah is with the doers of good."*[197] We need to constantly make *du'ā'* to Allah that Allah allows us to leave a beautiful legacy that will be of long-lasting benefit. We need to ask Him to accept our deeds and put *barakah* in them and set our sights high. Imām al-Bukhārī records that our Prophet ﷺ said, *"...if you ask Allah [for Jannah], then ask Him for al-Firdous..."*[198] Not everyone will get to *Firdous*, but we are all commanded to ask for it.

197 *al-'Ankabūt* 29: 69
198 *Ṣaḥīḥ* al-Bukharī 2790

www.ingramcontent.com/pod-product-compliance
Lightning Source LLC
Chambersburg PA
CBHW041307110526
44590CB00028B/4276
* 9 7 8 1 9 1 5 8 5 1 0 3 1 *